Ancient Democracy and Modern Ideology

DUCKWORTH CLASSICAL ESSAYS

Series editor:
Thomas Harrison, University of Liverpool

Ancient Democracy and Modern Ideology
Peter Rhodes

Interpreting Classical Texts
Malcolm Heath

The Invention of Ancient Slavery
Niall McKeown

Reading Cicero:
Genre and Performance in Late Republican Rome
Catherine Steel

DUCKWORTH CLASSICAL ESSAYS

Ancient Democracy
and
Modern Ideology

P.J. Rhodes

Duckworth

This impression 2007
First published in 2003 by
Gerald Duckworth & Co. Ltd.
90-93 Cowcross Street, London EC1M 6BF
Tel: 020 7490 7300
Fax: 020 7490 0080
inquiries@duckworth-publishers.co.uk
www.ducknet.co.uk

© 2003 by P.J. Rhodes

ISBN 978 0 7156 3220 8

Typeset by Ray Davies

Contents

Preface

In recent decades studies of ancient history overtly linked to an agenda in today's world have become respectable, as in the late nineteenth and early twentieth centuries they were not. Democracy, which for many centuries was condemned as mob rule, came to be seen positively in the nineteenth century and became the form of government in which almost everybody claimed to believe in the twentieth. The concept of democracy was first formulated in classical Greece, probably in Athens about the 460s BC, and in the fifth century Athens regarded itself and was regarded by others as an exemplar of democracy. In the modern world, those who first praised democracy praised Athenian democracy; more recently many have complained that Athens was not democratic enough, since its citizen body excluded women and children, immigrants and slaves, and in the fifth century acquired imperial power over other cities; defenders have stressed that it was normal rather than abnormal in its exclusions, and was much more successful at securing the active participation of those who were citizens than the representative democracies of the modern world. Particular attention was focused on Athenian democracy when, in 1993/4, the 2,500th anniversary of Cleisthenes' reforms was chosen as an occasion for major celebrations.

Preface

This book examines the ways in which Athenian democracy has been perceived and studied, over the centuries and particularly in recent times, and argues that, although total objectivity and disengagement are not and never have been possible, scholars who aspire to objectivity and disengagement are likely to do better history, and also to be more useful to our own world, than those who rejoice in their subjectivity and in their engagement with our world.

I am very grateful to Dr T.E.H. Harrison for inciting me to write this book and commenting on drafts of it, and to Duckworth for publishing it; to many friends for discussion and comments, in particular Dr R.W. Brock, Dr J. Ma, Dr L.G. Mitchell, Dr. L. Rubinstein, Prof. L.J. Samons, II, and Prof. A.C. Scafuro; and to audiences at Tübingen and Harvard Universities which listened and responded to a lecture based on it. I am grateful also for the opportunity to complete the book during a year of research leave and leave of absence from the University of Durham (where Mr G.J.C. Osborn took over my teaching), partly in Oxford, where as before I enjoyed the hospitality of Corpus Christi College, and where the new Sackler Library aided my work, and partly in Tallahassee, where I was honoured by the invitation to spend the spring semester of 2002 in the Department of Classics at Florida State University as Langford Family Eminent Scholar.

P.J.R.

1

History

History is made by people, in two senses.

Aristotle characterised history as the study of 'what Alcibiades did and what happened to him' (*Poetics* 9.1451b5-11). This characterisation is fair if we take it to cover not only major events and the lives of leading figures, such as the notorious late-fifth-century Athenian Alcibiades, but also ordinary figures and the events surrounding them, important individually only to those directly involved, but collectively helping us to build up a picture of life in a particular place at a particular time, and to see how it was similar to or different from life in other places at that time or in that place or other places at another time. We must also take it to cover not only people and events but every aspect of the conditions in which people lived their lives – including, for the purposes of this book, political ideas, such as beliefs about democracy; political machinery and the rules governing its working; informal political processes and their interaction with the formal processes. History is much more than a catalogue of names and events, but it is still fundamentally concerned with the lives which actual people actually lived in particular places at particular times.

History is made by people also in the sense that it is people who study history and who make of it what they can, a fact which has recently received a good deal of emphasis.[1] Interest in asking particular kinds of question, or in working with particular kinds of material; the context in which they work as historians (I, for instance, have always worked in a department of Classics, not in a department of History); a preference for intricate problems of detail or for wide-ranging explanation; the society in which they themselves live and their own kind of engagement with it – these factors and many others lead different historians to approach the same general area of history in different ways. History always involves some kind of interaction between the subject being studied and the historians studying it. A recent book on archaic Greece has been entitled, with suitable ambiguity, *Greece in the Making*,[2] because the archaic period in Greece was important in making the Greece of the classical period, because the later Greeks from whom we derive most of our knowledge of the archaic period were making versions of the archaic period to suit their own needs – and because the author of the book was making his version of the archaic period to suit present-day needs.

The world studied by historians is a pre-Einsteinian world, in which what has happened has happened and cannot be made to happen otherwise (though what has happened can, of course, be seen and interpreted in many different ways). Historical truths cannot satisfy the ultra-strict criteria for certainty laid down by the Logical Positivists in the first half of the twentieth century;[3] but for a myriad of factual questions there is a right answer. Sometimes the state of the evidence makes the right answer unobtainable (we do not know the year in which the Athenian Themistocles was ostracised); in other cases an answer is widely agreed to be probable but new evidence may show that after all that answer was wrong (it was agreed that the cave of Aglaurus in Athens was on the north side of the Acropolis until an inscription was found, indubitably in its original location, which showed far more certainly that the cave was at the east end of the Acropolis[4]); other answers are for all practical purposes totally certain (that Alexander the Great died at Babylon after a period of illness in 323, that Julius Caesar was killed at Rome on 15 March 44). We may disagree about the circumstances and interpretation of those deaths; we may speculate on how the world might have developed if they had not occurred as and when they did;[5] but we cannot bring into being an alternative world in which those deaths did not occur as and when they did, and the world did not subsequently develop as it did. Historians' reconstruction of the past is limited by what happened in the past (in the broad sense of 'happened' indicated above), in so far as what happened can be ascertained: where the answers are not certain, what we think likely to be right may depend partly on facts about ourselves, and that is something we need to be aware of; but where the answers are certain, or appear to be so, we cannot reject them, however inconvenient they may sometimes be for ourselves and for the picture of the past we are trying to elucidate.

So history was made by the people whom we study and by the sources which we study, and it is made by us as we study it, but we are not free to 'make it up' in whatever way we wish. There remains ample scope for individual approaches, to what material is studied, to what questions are asked of the material and to what kinds of answers to the questions are judged acceptable, and the best historians have always been conscious of this. In the late nineteenth and early twentieth centuries, in particular, many were tempted to see history as a *Wissenschaft* (science), which ought to try to bring to the study of its subject-matter the objectivity which *Naturwissenschaft* (natural science) was believed to bring to the study of its subject-matter. L. von Ranke proclaimed that 'Strict exposition of the facts, however qualified and unattractive it may yet be, is without doubt the highest law'; and in an often-quoted sentence he professed to tell it 'as it actually was'.[6] In context his telling it 'as it actually was' was to be contrasted with passing judgment on the past or providing instruction for the future; but the phrase was seized on, particularly in the USA, as a slogan for the would-be objective history which claims to eschew interpretative glosses and 'let the facts speak for themselves'. The *Cambridge Histories*, planned at the end of the nineteenth century and published from the beginning of the twentieth, were undertaken on the assumption that it is possible to write a definitive and totally objective history, that 'impartiality is the character of legitimate history' and 'the work is carried on by men [*sic*] acting together for no other object than the increase of accurate knowledge'.[7] The Greek historian Thucydides used to be admired because he was thought to approach as nearly as possible to that ideal.

Nowadays we are wiser (or think we are) but not necessarily sadder. Current fashion emphasises that because of the historians' own involvement there cannot be a scientific, objective and impartial history; those who are happy to be labelled post-modernists rejoice in historians' personal engagement and in the personal constructions of history which result from it, and suggest that one historian's construction has as much validity as another's (while nevertheless trying to indicate, the cynic may think, that their own constructions are good and their critics' are bad[8]). Thucydides is still admired, but it is acknowledged that, as a member of an anti-Periclean family who himself admired Pericles, and as an Athenian who held a command in the war and was exiled on account of it, he cannot be supposed to be impartial; both historians and specialists in historiography see him now not as a dispassionate chronicler of facts but as an 'artful reporter' who used literary devices to lead his readers to see things as he wanted.[9] His predecessor Herodotus has been accused of not having visited the places and seen the things which he claims to have visited and seen, and of having invented source references which are too good to be true as a literary device to achieve verisimilitude;[10] and one scholar has maintained that 'the notion of historical reality ... was foreign to the thinking of Graeco-Roman antiquity', that 'Herodotus does not look for the facts *behind* the traditions about them. ... There are only versions and no ultimate truth. ... He has no notion of getting at the *bare* facts, whatever that may mean. To him facts are always dressed.'[11]

Extremists may have taken this approach too far, but one gain that has undoubtedly been made in the past half-century is that, although our predecessors were far from naïve, we have become more aware of the dangers of supposing that a text can simply speak for itself, and of the various ways in which texts require interpretation.[12] Even so, this does not mean that we have unlimited freedom. We cannot summon the authors and ask what they meant in the texts, or summon their first readers and ask how they understood the texts, but one of our duties in studying the texts is to understand them in their contexts so that we can distinguish between interpretations which can credibly be attributed to the authors and to their first readers and interpretations which cannot. Beyond that, there are of course significances other than those originally intended or perceived which can validly be discovered when a text is read in another context;[13] but, just as we are not free to make whatever we like of past people and their lives, we are not free to read whatever we like in their texts. In an earlier age J. Ruskin could proclaim confidently, 'At least be sure that you go to the author to get at *his* meaning, not to find yours':[14] that should still be our aim, even if we are more conscious than our predecessors of the difficulty of achieving it.[15]

I must add here that, although the ancient historians were not exactly like modern academic historians, they were still historians; the best of them tried seriously to discover and explain what had happened in the past, and among the arguments which they used in doing so were arguments of the kind which we still regard as appropriate to historians.[16]

In the study of how historians have worked which we may call metahistory,[17] just as in history, simple explanations are in danger of being over-simple; but it may be suggested that Marxism has played an important part in the change from objectivity to subjectivity. In the middle of the twentieth century many historians displayed a degree of sympathy with Marxism which made it possible for critics to claim that their work was ideologically driven; they tended to respond to their attackers by insisting that all scholars are ideologically driven,

14

and that those who do not admit to it are more naïve and / or more dangerous than those who do.[18] Thus, after a period in which it was normal to profess objectivity and impartiality, being ideologically driven and studying history with one's eye on an agenda in the modern world became respectable.

It still remains true that some scholars react to their inevitable subjectivity by keeping it in the background, trying to recognise and allow for their prejudices while seeking to understand their subject-matter on its own terms, and often gravitating to investigations of a kind in which the scope for the investigator's subjectivity is limited: there is not much opportunity for historians to be led or misled by their own ideology in attempting to locate the demes of Attica on the map and to decide whether they were grouped in equal *trittyes* or unequal *trittyes*.[19] Others rejoice in their own subjectivity and in the claim that their critics are no less subjective, insist that they are studying history not just as a collection of obscure facts but in order to make it relevant to the world they live in,[20] and often gravitate to investigations of a kind where the part played by value-judgments is more significant. In the heyday of Marxism a good deal of time and energy were devoted, both by sympathisers with and by opponents of Marxism, to the subject of slavery in Athens and in the ancient world generally.[21] There are many factual questions, concerning how many Athenians owned how many slaves, what use they made of them and how they treated them, to which there should in principle be right answers; many of the right answers cannot be securely established for lack of evidence, though people have done their best with the material that we have. But connected with those are more emotive questions, concerning how the Athenians (and how the slaves) thought about slavery, how far Athens was a 'slave society' in which the citizens were free to engage in civic political and cultural activities only because they had slaves to do the menial work which they would otherwise have had to do for themselves, how far the Athenians whom we admire for being democratic ought rather to be condemned because their democracy was limited to adult males of Athenian ancestry and depended on the repression and exploitation of others. Or rather of Others, with a capital O; since at the end of the twentieth century and the beginning of the twenty-first the focus has been on the contrast between those who belong and Others of various kinds who do not, among whom slaves are less discussed than in the past and women are now prominent.[22]

That historians want to make the Greek and Roman world intelligible and interesting to inhabitants of our own world, that different historians approach the Greek and Roman world with different interests and from different standpoints, can only be good. Because of our ignorance, and because of the differences between their ideas and ours, we can never wholly understand the Greeks and Romans; we may find some things easy to understand which students in other times and other places have found hard to understand, and *vice versa*; we are likely to understand more if we have access to and allow ourselves to be stimulated by a variety of approaches. And it may profit us – not only in our study of the ancient world but also in our engagement with our own world – if we are stimulated to think about similarities and dissimilarities between the world we are studying and our own world, both by studies which overtly set out to stimulate such thought and by studies which do not.

But I end this chapter by returning to my insistence that, although our perspective may change, we cannot alter what happened in the past. We are dealing with people who lived and died, who did things, who thought, said and wrote things and who had things done to them; communities which existed and which prospered or failed to prosper; events and processes which occurred; and a body of evidence which requires interpretation but which cannot be twisted so as to mean whatever we want it to mean. Making the past intelligible and interesting to us in the present requires us not only to do justice to our own needs but also to do justice to the people whom we are studying and to the material which we are studying; and, if we allow ourselves to be so preoccupied with the present that we cease doing that, we cease being historians.

2

Democracy

Demo-kratia, 'people-power', had become a controversial subject by the second half of the fifth century BC. In the polarisation of the Greek states between Athens and Sparta which led to the Peloponnesian War of 431-404, Athens was democratic, encouraged or required democratic constitutions among her allies (e.g. Erythrae in the late 450s, Miletus not later than 435[1]) and was perceived as a champion of democracy; Sparta was not a typical oligarchy but was an idiosyncratic state in which there was a considerable measure of political equality within an exceptionally restricted citizen body, but it tended to prefer oligarchic constitutions among its allies and was perceived as a champion of oligarchy. Herodotus, probably writing in the 440s-420s, insistently but implausibly locates a debate on the rival merits of democracy, oligarchy and monarchy in the Persian Empire in the 520s (III.80-3 cf. VI.43.iii). One conclusion to which the relativism of the sophists, the intellectuals active in Athens and elsewhere in the late fifth century, could lead was that there is no absolutely best form of constitution but different forms suit different people: the writer called by Gilbert Murray the 'Old Oligarch',[2] probably in the 420s, regarded democracy as distasteful but at Athens successful and stable; at the beginning of the fourth century a client of the orator Lysias, accepting the relativist doctrine, to support the argument that he was not implicated in Athens' late-fifth-century bouts of oligarchy insisted that he was not a man to whom an oligarchic régime would be advantageous (Lysias XXV).

Herodotus and the Old Oligarch, if correctly dated above, are the earliest attested users of the word *demokratia*.[3] The Athenians were self-consciously democratic at the latest when they imposed a democratic constitution on Erythrae, in the late 450s, but there is no reason to believe that the actual word was used in the decree ordering that constitution. A version of the threefold classification of constitutions used by Herodotus is to be found in Pindar, *Pythian* ii.86-8, perhaps of 468;[4] and we perhaps see the word *demokratia* recently coined or about to be coined in the reference to the *demou kratousa cheir* ('powerful hand of the people') for an assembly (in Argos in the heroic period) voting by show of hands in Aeschylus, *Suppliants* 604, probably of 464/3. Some have wanted to see the word in use already at the time of Cleisthenes' reforms in Athens, in 508/7. More probably the language used then was the language of 'equality' (our evidence suggests that various compounds of *iso-* were current then); discussion of how states ought to be governed, and the word *demokratia*, surfaced in Athens in the 460s; Ephialtes and his supporters in 462/1 were the first reformers who claimed explicitly to be democratic – and *oligarchia* was coined subsequently as a label for régimes which were not democratic.[5]

The Greek word *demos* was ambiguous, like the English 'people'. It could be used either of the whole community, including the privileged few as well as the unprivileged many, or specifically of the unprivileged many, in contrast to the privileged few: both senses can be found as early as the poetry of Solon of Athens, at the beginning of the sixth century, e.g. in fr. 36 West quoted by [Aristotle], *Athenian Constitution* 12.iv the first sense, probably, in l. 2 but the second sense, certainly, in l. 25. *Demokratia* could therefore be represented as the entrusting of political power either to the whole people, as in Pericles' funeral oration in Thucydides II.37.i, or to the poor majority, as in [Xenophon], *Athenian Constitution* i.2-5 and *passim*. Aristotle in book III of his *Politics* begins with a purely numerical classification of rule by one man or a few or many, as in Herodotus' Persian debate, while distinguishing in each case between a good version in which the rulers aim for the common good and a bad in which they pursue their own sectional interests; but he then turns to an economic distinction between (bad) oligarchy as the rule of the rich and (bad) democracy as the rule of the poor (*Politics* III.1278b6-1279b10, 1279b11-1280a6). One means which was used to enable constitutions which were democratic in theory to work democratically in practice, with poor citizens as well as rich playing an active part, was the provision of modest salaries for the performance of civic functions like holding office, serving on juries and attending meetings of the assembly. The earliest such payment to be attested is the payment to jurors in Athens, probably introduced in the 450s ([Aristotle], *Athenian Constitution* 27.iii-iv). One reason for Athens' oligarchic revolution in 411 was that Athens was short of money, rich citizens did not need to be paid and so most of these salaries could be abolished (Thucydides VIII.67.iii, [Aristotle], *Athenian Constitution* 29.v); and Aristotle remarked that democracies pay

2. Democracy

men for attendance while oligarchies fine men for non-atten-
dance (e.g. *Politics* IV.1294a37-b1); but it appears that even in
the moderately oligarchic Boeotia of the late fifth and early
fourth centuries members of the federal council had their
living expenses paid (*Hellenica Oxyrhynchia* 19.iv Chambers).[6]

We must remember also that Greek states, even when democratic, regularly contained inhabitants who were not citizens,
not true members of the *demos* at all. Children of citizens (as
still in our world), and adult daughters and wives of citizens
(as no longer in our world, but still regularly until the twentieth century), were members of citizen families but were not
themselves citizens with political rights. But there could also
be free non-citizens (known in Athens as *metoikoi*, 'metics',
i.e. migrants): citizenship was normally inherited from citizen
parents, and, although a man who changed his city of resi-
dence might be rewarded with citizenship for some special
benefaction, neither the original migrant nor his descendants
often had the right to apply for citizenship. And there were
also, as I have already mentioned, slaves: in some places,
native people in a special form of servitude, of whom the
Spartan helots (a word probably meaning 'captives') are the
best-known example; in many places chattel slaves, usually
non-Greek, who might in theory be protected at least against
being killed by their owners, and who might in some contexts
be reasonably well treated, but who had virtually no rights.
Some slaves were eventually liberated by their owners: in the
Roman world, which in any case saw a great expansion of the
citizen body over the centuries, liberated slaves became citizens, but in the Greek world they became metics. Democrats

were no more likely than oligarchs to want to extend citizenship beyond the sons of citizen parents: indeed it was the democrats in Athens who in 451/0 tightened the qualification for citizenship, requiring an Athenian mother as well as an Athenian father ([Aristotle], *Athenian Constitution* 26.iv).

In practice, a democratic state could differ from an oligarchic in two main ways. First, a democratic state would give basic political rights, at least membership of the decision-making citizen assembly and of juries, to all free men of local ancestry, though it might impose a (not necessarily high) property qualification for holding offices (democratic Athens did that: the property qualification was still enforced in the fifth century, was retained in law but was no longer enforced in the fourth: [Aristotle], *Athenian Constitution* 7.iii-8.i, 47.i). An oligarchic state would make the exercise of any political rights subject to a property qualification (as in both the individual cities of Boeotia and the federation in which they were combined: *Hellenica Oxyrhynchia* 19.ii Chambers). Secondly, although the practice of *probouleusis*,[7] decision-making by an assembly of citizens after prior deliberation by a smaller council, was widespread among Greek states of various complexions, a democracy was likely to tip the balance so that the assembly was comparatively strong and the council and individual officials were comparatively weak (in democratic Athens the council fixed the assembly's agenda, but a great many decisions were taken by the assembly, and once a matter reached the assembly any citizen could make a proposal or speak), but an oligarchy was likely to tip the balance the other way (in this respect Sparta was oligarchic: an assembly of the limited citizen body had the last word in making major decisions, but it did not decide as many matters as in Athens; and it appears that only the two hereditary kings, the five annual officials called ephors and the members of the small council of elders known as the *gerousia* could speak in the assembly, and the assembly could only vote for or against a proposal submitted to it by the *gerousia*). In Athens in 411-410 the extreme oligarchic régime of the Four Hundred took the oligarchic line on both of those points; it is arguable that the intermediate régime of the Five Thousand which followed retained the oligarchic limitation of the citizen body but returned to the strong assembly of the democracy.[8]

By the second half of the twentieth century it had become almost universally agreed that democracy is the best form of constitution, and different kinds of régime adjusted the definition of democracy so that the word could be applied to their form of government. That was not the case, as we shall see, in earlier periods of modern history, and it was not the case, as we have already seen, in classical Greek history. Many Greeks were happy to argue that democracy was not in their interests as individuals, or on general grounds that democracy is not the best form of constitution – in particular because they thought that political decision-making like other tasks is one that calls for expertise (e.g. Plato, *Republic* IV.427e-429a) or because they thought that those who have a greater stake in the community through owning more of its property[9] and fighting in its army deserve to have a greater say in the running of the community (an argument set up for attack by Athenagoras of Syracuse in Thucydides VI.39.i). Aristotle, though not a believer in extreme democracy, countered those arguments by suggesting that the many may collectively be better at making decisions than superior individuals, and may collectively own more of the community's property than rich individuals (*Politics* III.1281a39-1282b13). It was possible to distinguish between a respectable oligarchy (one which was *isonomos*, 'fair' or 'equal' in its laws) and an irresponsible clique (*dynasteia*) of a few men, 'contrary to laws and good sense and close to tyranny' (Thucydides III.62.iii). The intermediate régime of the Five Thousand which ruled Athens in 411/0 between the fall of the Four Hundred and the restoration of the democracy (cf. above) was admired by Thucydides, who describes it as 'a reasonable mixture with regard to the few and the many' (VIII.97.ii).

In the hellenistic period, between the death of Alexander the Great in 323 and the Roman conquest of the Greek world in the second and first centuries, there was something of a change. Most states had the kind of structures which could have been reasonably democratic if the poorer citizens were both permitted by law and enabled in practice to play an active part. All too often we are unable to discover whether those conditions were satisfied, though in the few cases where we have voting figures which we can set against estimates of population they point to assemblies not limited by a property qualification. Otherwise, in the Greek heartland – that is, the Greek mainland, the Aegean islands and the westernmost part of Asia Minor – signs of active involvement by a good number of citizens remain reasonably frequent for a reasonable time, but in 'Greek' cities elsewhere, whether old-established colonies in the west or new foundations in Asia, they are rarer. It was always possible for rich individuals who were prepared to spend their own money on the performance of civic duties to satisfy their ambition and to gratify their cities by doing so. Overall there was a tendency, encouraged in due course by the Romans, for the part played by the rich in the running of their cities to increase, but that development seems to have been neither as rapid nor as uniform as used to be believed. As for the language, there seems to have been a bifurcation. Sometimes democracy still means what it meant in the classical period, and is seriously contrasted with oligarchy; but in other texts democracy means what it sometimes meant in Herodotus, and can refer to any kind of constitutional government in contrast to tyranny.[10]

When we study democracy in the Greek world we focus primarily on the classical period of the fifth and fourth centuries, and especially on Athens. As we have seen, it was probably in Athens that the concept of democracy was formulated, and it is certain that by the middle of the fifth century Athens was self-consciously democratic, and saw itself and was seen by others as a champion of democracy. A further reason for focusing on classical Athens is that we are exceptionally well informed about it: from the 450s the Athenian democracy seems to have had a deliberate policy of keeping the citizens informed, and took to inscribing documents on stone on a scale not matched by any other Greek state; and in the fifth and fourth centuries (though not earlier or later) Athens was the cultural centre of the Greek world, so that a very large proportion of the Greek literature that survives from those centuries was written by Athenians or else by non-Athenians working in Athens. And there is one partly accidental survival.[11] The school of the philosopher Aristotle (one of the non-Athenians working in Athens) made a collection of 158 constitutions: none of them has survived through the western manuscript tradition, but an almost complete text of the *Athenian Constitution* survived on papyrus in Egypt, and was first read and published in 1891. The first two thirds give a history of the constitution to the end of the fifth century (derived partly from Herodotus and Thucydides but largely from sources which do not themselves now survive), and the remaining third gives an account of the working of the constitution in the author's own time (essentially the 330s, but our text has a few revisions made in the 320s).

3

Democracy: Good or Bad?

That attitudes to ancient democracy should be conditioned by the circumstances of people in their own world is no novelty.[1] Over many centuries education in the Classics was available particularly to the clergy before the Reformation and to the gentry after, i.e. to people who would not necessarily approve of giving political power to the *demos*. The Bible could be quoted in support of monarchy (Mark xii.13-17, Matthew xxii.15-22; Romans xiii.1-7), and Aquinas had pronounced in favour of monarchy (e.g. *De Regimine Principum*, I.ii / 16-20). The first texts on Greek democracy to be rediscovered in the west were Aristotle's *Politics*, in which democracy is one of the bad forms of constitution, and the essay of the Old Oligarch, disapproving of democracy in Athens. Plutarch was influential, and his *Lives* often led to the view that Athens was at its best under Solon, at the beginning of the sixth century, and became steadily worse thereafter; but for a long time Athens attracted less interest than Sparta or Rome. There was a period in the fifteenth century when Florence saw itself as a second Athens (not for its form of government but for being a city state which stood up to the great powers as Athens had stood up to Philip of Macedon); but from Machiavelli[2] in the early

27

sixteenth century onwards attitudes to democracy were generally hostile.

The first moves away from absolute monarchy in the late mediaeval and modern periods did not rely on ancient precedents, and for a long time the usual aim was not to do away with monarchs but simply to limit their power, particularly their power to levy taxes: freedom from despotism was what was wanted, not power for the people. Thus in Switzerland 'we must not too hastily salute in [the confederation of 1394] the triumph of liberal or democratic principles. The freedom for which the cantons had fought was their own communal independence, not "the freedom of the individual in the state and from the state".' Although a contrast can be drawn between the rural cantons with their assemblies (*Landsgemeinde*)[3] and the cities with their oligarchies, 'in the early history of all the forest cantons there are traces of a directing élite, and sometimes an aristocracy of birth'.[4] In seventeenth-century England what was at issue was the power of Parliament, as representative of the People, and indeed whether the monarchy should merely have its power limited or should be abolished.[5] In January 1649 the House of Commons resolved that 'The People are, under God, the Original of all just Power. ... The Commons of England, in Parliament assembled, being chosen by and representing the People, have the supreme Power in this Nation.'[6] In March the Commons abolished the office of King, and the house of Lords; in May they resolved that 'the people of England ... shall from henceforth be governed as a Commonwealth and Free State by the supreme authority of this nation, the representatives of the people in Parliament, and by such as they shall appoint and constitute as officers and ministers under them for the good of the people'.[7] Among the supporters of the Commonwealth was John Milton, who was an accomplished classicist, and he did indeed in his political works include some examples and quotations from Greece and Rome.[8]

In the eighteenth century the Founding Fathers of the USA used ancient history to support their views, but they do not seem to have derived their views from ancient history, and they owed more to modern books than to ancient texts and translations of them.[9] They found some things to praise in democratic Athens, but more to worry them; they admired Sparta for its stability; they were interested in Greek federal organisations but did not know much about them; but they were more interested in Rome and the concept of a republic, and in particular they focused on the need for a representative system and separation of powers to save them from the excesses of democracy.[10] In the constitution of 1787 there are a few echoes of Rome, none of Greece. In France Louis de Jaucourt in the *Encyclopédie* provided a reasonably favourable treatment of democracy: 'Although I do not think democracy is the most convenient and the most stable form of government', it is ancient and respectable; the purest form of democracy is a direct democracy; democracy can be corrupted in either of two directions, by losing the spirit of equality or by taking it to extremes.[11] Voltaire praised Athens in the article on 'démocratie' in the *Dictionnaire philosophique*.[12] In 1788 C. de Pauw was surprisingly pro-Athenian and anti-Spartan in his *Philosophical Dissertations on the Greeks* – but in the same year the usual anti-Athenian picture was given in J.J. Barthélemy's *Travels of Anacharsis the Younger in Greece*.[13]

The French revolution was inspired more by Rome – by Brutus and Cato and the idea of resistance to tyranny. The Jacobins liked Sparta; ancient history provided some glorious martyr-doms of republican heroes; the most pro-Athenian writer was Camille Desmoulins in his journal *Le Vieux Cordelier*.[14]

Britain had lost America and was alarmed by France: the best known of many anti-democratic British books is William Mitford's *History of Greece*,[15] of which it has been said that 'it was Mitford who more than anyone else legitimized the use of Athenian history for debating in detail the wisdom and viabil-ity of modern democratic government'.[16] Thomas Paine, who visited France and America, was one of the first writers to use the word 'democracy' favourably. He declared that 'Though the ancient governments present to us a miserable picture of the condition of man, there is one which above all others exempts itself from the general description. I mean the demo-cracy of the Athenians.' However, he let the Americans persuade him that 'representation ingrafted upon democracy' was better.[17] This concept of 'representative democracy' had appeared in the eighteenth century in William Blackstone's *Commentaries on the Laws of England*. The House of Com-mons was the 'democratic' part of the constitution, and for a large and populous state representation was better than direct participation:[18]

> In a free state, every man, who is supposed a free agent, ought to be, in some measure, his own governor; and therefore a branch at least of the legislative power should reside in the whole body of the people. And this power, when the territories of the state are small and it's [*sic*]

30

3. Democracy: Good or Bad?

citizens easily known, should be exercised by the people in their aggregate or collective capacity, as was widely ordained in the petty republics of Greece, and the first rudiments of the Roman state. But this will be highly inconvenient, when the public territory is extended to any considerable degree, and the number of citizens is encreased. ... In so large a state as ours it is therefore very wisely contrived, that the people should do that by their representatives, which it is impracticable to perform in person. [p. 154] ... Next, with regard to the elections of knights, citizens and burgesses; we may observe that herein consists the exercise of the democratical part of our constitution: for in a democracy there can be no exercise of sovereignty but by suffrage, which is the declaration of the people's will. [p. 164]

In the nineteenth century, when Alexis de Tocqueville travelled from France to study America, he focused on American representative democracy and tried to see both good and bad in it. In looking at the conflict between individual freedom and the dominance of the majority, he feared that the end might be either a totalitarian tyranny of the majority or else anarchy; and he noted what a small proportion of the inhabitants of Athens were citizens: 'Athens, then, with her universal suffrage, was after all merely an aristocratic republic in which all the nobles had an equal right to the government.'[19]

Eighteenth-century Germany provided an unexpected stimulus for valuing Athens above Sparta, when J.J. Winckelmann admired Athens' achievement in the visual arts and was led to think that the Athens in which the arts flourished must have been better than the Sparta in which they did not.[20] In Britain the tide turned in the second quarter of the nineteenth century. Thomas Macaulay in 1824 published both an enthusiastic essay 'On the Athenian Orators' and a pro-democratic review of Mitford's *History* (complaining, 'He is a vehement admirer of tyranny and oligarchy. ... Democracy he hates with a perfect hatred').[21] Another pro-democratic response to Mitford was produced in 1826 by George Grote, and the first edition of Grote's *History of Greece* was published between 1846 and 1856.[22] Grote had had to follow his father into banking instead of going to Oxford or Cambridge; he was a friend and disciple of James Mill, the father of John Stuart Mill; he was one of the leading figures behind the foundation of London University. His *History of Greece* was perhaps the first history of Greece which we can still recognise as a work of what we should understand as serious scholarship, and it purveyed a favourable view of democratic Athens which was not accepted by everybody[23] but after which things could never be the same again. Macaulay wanted to take Athens out of the debate about current politics; Grote wanted to keep Athens in the debate, but as a positive rather than negative model,[24] and since then it has been common, among his detractors as well as his supporters, to believe that Greek history in general, and Athenian democracy in particular, is not only a subject for academic investigation but is relevant to us in confronting the problems of our own world.

However, it was only in the twentieth century, and particularly the second half of that century, that democracy changed from being a form of government which could be admired to being the one form of government which almost everybody claims to admire: now almost all governments profess to embody democracy and almost all people active in or writing about politics profess to approve of it – and they then redefine the term in order to apply it to whatever form of government they actually prefer.

Views of democratic Athens have never been separable from the political and moral attitudes of the people holding those views; but after Grote it becomes possible to write of scholarship, and in the remainder of this book I wish to concentrate on how democracy and scholarship have interacted and whether there is a point beyond which such interaction is undesirable.

4

Democracy: Fashions in Scholarship

Since the time of Grote, the part played by Greece and Rome in education has declined, while scholarship has become more specialised and more professional. In the First World War quotations from Pericles' funeral oration in Thucydides were displayed on London buses;[1] but the last British Prime Minister to have been educated as a classicist and to have continued reading books on Greece and Rome in his spare time was Harold Macmillan, and I doubt if quotations from a Greek source would be judged suitable for upholding public morale today. But I turn to the work of professional scholars.[2]

The working of the machinery

We have seen that to some extent history is bound to be what historians make of it; that some historians try to minimise their personal engagement and push it into the background while others take pride in it. In the heyday of scholarship as *Wissenschaft*, at the end of the nineteenth century and the beginning of the twentieth, what seemed to be the professional approach to Athenian democracy and to ancient forms of government in general was to study *Staatsaltertümer* ('constitutional antiquities'). This kind of work had begun in the first half of the

34

4. Democracy: Fashions in Scholarship

nineteenth century with G.F. Schoemann, who published *De Comitiis Atheniensium Libri Tres* ('Three Books on the Athenian Assemblies') in 1819; in 1817 his contemporary A. Boeckh had published the *Staatshaushaltung der Athener* ('The Public Economy of Athens'),[3] which has been described as 'the first book on a Greek subject which used inscriptions freely not as curiosities but as integral parts of the evidence'.[4] In the second half of the century T. Mommsen led the way on the Roman side with his *Römisches Staatsrecht* ('Roman Constitutional Law');[5] and for Athens and all the Greek states the literary and epigraphic sources were meticulously combed for facts which could be set in order. The appearance of the Aristotelian *Athenian Constitution* in 1891 gave a great boost to work of this kind, and the crowning glory of this form of scholarship was the *Griechische Staatskunde* ('Greek Constitutional Study') of G. Busolt, the last edition of which was completed after his death by H. Swoboda.[6]

Those Germans who were not content to catalogue antiquities but expressed opinions tended to be hostile to Athenian democracy: it will be sufficient to cite E. Meyer on Grote as a partisan writer;[7] Wilamowitz approved of the Athenians' empire but not of their democracy.[8] In the Nazi period it was Sparta that particularly attracted approval, and especially the sacrificial death of the Spartans at Thermopylae.[9]

The *Staatskunde* tradition continued with people who were still essentially asking, 'What was the machinery and how did it work?' though taking a slightly broader view of what asking that might involve. U. Kahrstedt was described by one reviewer as starting not with the data but with a questionnaire:[10] he liked legality; he liked firm answers, and he sometimes forced the evidence or the lack of it to obtain the answers which he wanted. He gave the title *Griechisches Staatsrecht* ('Greek Constitutional Law'), i, to a book on Sparta and the Peloponnesian League; but the economic problems of the 1920s and 1930s prevented the publication of his second volume, on Athens and its leagues:[11] eventually he published two volumes of 'Studien zum öffentlichen Recht Athens' ('Studies in Athenian Public Law'): *Staatsgebiet und Staats-angehörige in Athen* ('The State's Territory and the State's Members in Athens'), *Untersuchungen zur Magistratur in Athen* ('Investigations into Magistracies in Athens'); and they were followed by a series of articles under the general heading 'Untersuchungen zu athenischen Behörden' ('Investigations into Athenian Offices').[12] V. Ehrenberg, whose career began in Germany and ended in the United Kingdom, published *Der griechische und der hellenistische Staat* ('The Greek and Hellenistic State') in 1932, and two revised editions, each in both German and English versions, after the Second World War.[13] He took material from Athens, Sparta and elsewhere to discuss the *polis* in general, and treated units larger than the *polis* as well as the *polis*, and the hellenistic period as well as the classical; he stressed that 'The Polis was the state of the *politai*, the citizens' (2nd English ed., p. 88); he was not hard on the demagogues, and 'we should not judge [slavery] in a Pharisaic spirit' (p. 97); his strongest criticism was of the Athenian law courts: 'Democracy reached its perfection by making the people judges of everything; but in doing so, it brought grave discredit upon itself' (p. 74).

C. Meier, who began with Roman politics and has extended his interest to Greek, has written on *The Greek Discovery of*

4. Democracy: Fashions in Scholarship

Politics:[14] the book is addressed to readers with an interest in the modern world, omits material on democracy, economics and slaves because he was not yet ready to publish that, and remarks that 'we may be tempted, on grounds of mere numbers, to call the extreme democracy of Athens an oligarchy, since the free and equal who enjoyed full political rights were a small minority beside metics, slaves, and women. But this is to apply modern criteria' (English translation, p. 154). J. Bleicken's *Die athenische Demokratie*[15] of 1985 combines a factual account of the history and working of the democracy with a discussion of the nature of the democracy and the principles underlying it, stressing the exclusion of non-citizens and the reduced opportunities for citizens who lived at a distance from Athens and / or had to work for their living, and suggesting that the fourth century saw a decline not in the democracy's institutions but in the citizens' involvement.

In France, H. Francotte published *La Polis grecque* in 1907, which has been described as 'a number of useful essays, bundled together rather unorganically'.[16] In 1909 A. Croiset published in *Les Démocraties antiques* four chapters on Athens followed by one on other cities in Greece and one on Carthage and Rome: his view of Athens, both in the fifth century and in the fourth, was strongly favourable, including his view of Athens' treatment of slaves, women and the Delian League; his chief criticisms were of the volatility of the assembly and the prevalence of bribery.[17] More importantly, in 1928 G. Glotz published *La Cité grecque et ses institutions*.[18] It began with Homer and the origins of the *polis*, and ended with what Glotz saw as a decline in the fourth century; at its heart was an account of the working of the Athenian democracy, not a dry catalogue of facts but a rhetorical account not afraid of expressing approval or disapproval. In contrast to the Germans, he found more to praise than to blame in fifth-century Athens, and men like Cleon were at least judged to be men whose private interests coincided with those of the state; but in the fourth century he saw an excess of indivualism and the collapse of the family – his first book had been *La Solidarité de la famille dans le droit criminel en Grèce* ('The Solidarity of the Family in Criminal Law in Greece') – and apart from a few 'statesmen' political leaders were 'a despicable mob'. The triumph of Philip of Macedon was a defeat for the forces of progress (that being a *riposte* to German scholars who admired the Macedonian monarchy). It is worth noting that Glotz was Jewish. There was a tendency at that time in the anti-Semitic right in France to attack democracy and its tolerance of 'metics': C. Maurras, the founder of the movement Action Française, referred to 'our internal foreigners, Jews, metics or others', and proclaimed that 'the government of the multitude is in essence pernicious'.[19] More recently, French approaches to ancient politics have been coloured by the authors' positions *vis-à-vis* fascism and communism.[20] The ideas of Maurras have persisted, with a new twist: N. Loraux draws attention to a speech delivered in the National Assembly on 2 May 1990 by the National Front representative M.-F. Stirbois, which enlisted Athens' criteria for citizenship on the side of those hostile to immigrants – and even misleadingly cited Glotz in support of that position.[21] Recently, P. Vidal-Naquet has contrasted the freedom to be participants in Athenian democracy with the freedom to be consumers in modern western democracies, and has lamented the lack of proper consultation and debate in the construction of the European Union.[22]

British scholars did not particularly focus on Athenian democracy in the earlier part of the twentieth century. At the turn of the century A.H.J. Greenidge produced a pair of Greek and Roman constitutional handbooks in the German manner;[23] otherwise continental books were translated into English: the volume devoted to Sparta and Athens of G. Gilbert's *Handbuch der griechischen Staatsalterthümer* ('Handbook of Greek Constitutional Antiquities'),[24] and Glotz's *La Cité grecque*.[25] Writers of general books tended to express approval of Athenian democracy – like Glotz, in the fifth century but not in the fourth[26] – but the arch-conservative G.B. Grundy maintained that the battle of Marathon in 490 was not a triumph of democratic Athens but it was the 'democratic party' that favoured capitulation to the Persians; 'democracy proved itself jealous of its greatest children', and it was 'intensely communistic', being based on the poor citizens, competing against slave labour, who sought control of the state in their own class interests.[27]

In the 1920s M. Cary published an article on 'Athenian Democracy', in which he argued that 'the strictures passed on Athenian democracy contain much truth, but on the whole are too severe', though 'the suppression of the expert' made the Athenian form of democracy unsuitable for our world; the citizen body was restricted but was compulsorily involved, resulting in a 'khaki democracy' of men who fought for the state and wanted a say in running it.[28]

In 1949 A.W. Gomme gave a lecture to the Hellenic Society on 'The Working of the Athenian Democracy',[29] in which he stressed the power of the assembly and the importance but powerlessness of the council – and concluded that the Athenians were aware of the weaknesses of their system but still liked it. In 1957 R.J. Hopper gave his inaugural lecture at Sheffield on *The Basis of the Athenian Democracy*: he started with Aristotle, thought the demagogues were not necessarily worse than the generals, and stressed the involvement of the ordinary citizens, at the local level as well as the *polis* level. But most influential from that generation was the *Athenian Democracy* of A.H.M. Jones.[30] This combined four papers published a few years earlier (including his Cambridge inaugural lecture of 1952 on 'The Athens of Demosthenes'[31]) with a new paper, 'How Did the Athenian Democracy Work?' Jones criticised those who unthinkingly accepted the criticisms of upper-class ancient writers; he played down the dependence of the democracy on Athens' fifth-century empire and on slaves; like Gomme he emphasised the extent to which the Athenians in the assembly governed themselves – and one reader described the book as displaying 'mildly socialist leanings'.[32] And I should mention C. Hignett's *A History of the Athenian Constitution*, the published version of lectures given over many years at Oxford, which is mostly a diachronic history and was motivated more by a sceptical approach to post-fifth-century sources and by admiration for the German K.J. Beloch and the Italian G. de Sanctis than by any obvious political views: ch. ix gives an account of the 'radical democracy', claiming that the Athenians 'had a special aptitude for the successful working of popular government' (p. 250) and the maturity to trust statesmanlike leaders, and ch. x characterises 'the rule of the demagogues' as 'the divorce between influence and responsibility' (p. 264).

Subsequently P.J. Rhodes in *The Athenian Boule* continued in the tradition of asking how Athenian democratic institutions worked: this and other books provoked the response from W.R. Connor (a scholar who has paraded his own engagement with the modern world) that 'the study of this subject seems to require *little more* than the ancestral virtues. One need not move from the terra firma of constitutional history into the grim quick sands of social history.'[33] Rhodes went on to apply the ancestral virtues to a *Commentary on the Aristotelian Athenaion Politeia*; and then joined D.M. Lewis in a study of *The Decrees of the Greek States*, which was an investigation of 'how did it work?' updating for a much larger body of evidence the work done on inscriptions by H. Swoboda at the end of the nineteenth century, and joining a growing reaction against the view that the triumph of Philip II of Macedon over the Greek *poleis* in the fourth century represented 'the failure of the Greek *polis*' and 'the destruction of Greek democracy'.[34] He has also written on political activity in Athens.[35]

In the 1980s the question 'how did it work?' was asked at the local level in books on the Athenian demes by R. Osborne and D. Whitehead.[36] Osborne in a separate paper praised the solidarity and stability of the Athenian democracy, suggesting that it was due in part to the great variety of sub-units in the city which echoed the organisation of the city itself, so that there were opportunities for all the citizens to involve themselves in democratic processes in bodies which they found congenial.[37] The idea of involvement was crucial also for a

41

book written by an Australian, R.K. Sinclair's *Democracy and Participation in Athens*, which while doubling as a general handbook on Athens' democratic constitution focuses on the participation of the citizens and the role of leaders in the democracy: at the end the book acknowledges the exploitation of women, slaves and the subject allies, but gives a generally positive picture, and defends the democracy against its critics.[38]

Another scholar who has devoted a great deal of attention to the question 'how did it work?' is M.H. Hansen of Copenhagen. He has focused on the assembly and the lawcourts rather than the council and the generals; and to illuminate the working of the assembly he has studied the *Landsgemeinde* of some of the Swiss cantons. His earliest work was on Athenian law-suits of a political kind.[39] He then turned his attention to a whole range of questions concerning the working of the Athenian assembly, culminating in a book, *The Athenian Assembly in the Age of Demosthenes*, after which he produced the more general *The Athenian Democracy in the Age of Demosthenes*. He has concentrated on the fourth century, because that is the period for which we have the best evidence, and has argued that fourth-century Athenians deliberately adopted a less extreme version of democracy than their fifth-century predecessors.[40] More recently, like Rhodes, he has been looking at the Greek world as a whole, and is directing the researches of the Copenhagen Polis Centre: the Centre has embarked on the neo-Aristotelian project of compiling a catalogue of the known *poleis* of the archaic and classical periods and answering a series of factual questions about each, in order to achieve a better understanding of what a *polis* was.[41] At the

4. Democracy: Fashions in Scholarship

same time, he has been interested in the concepts of the state and of democracy, in the ancient world and in the modern, and has been more inclined than some other scholars to stress the similarity between Athenian *demokratia* and modern democracy.[42] But, although he has shown that kind of interest in the modern world and the relevance to it of the ancient, he is in the tradition of scholars who seek to understand the ancient world without pursuing an overt agenda in the modern world.

J. Ober in a review article on Hansen's *The Athenian Assembly*[43] criticised Hansen from the standpoint of one who believes that all historians have an ideology, including / especially those who think they have not: Hansen is concerned with 'narrowly focused and (to the non-specialist) often abstruse constitutional issues. ... His conclusions appear objective. ... But adopting certain of H.'s conclusions entails acquiescing in his specific understanding of political life.' Ober claimed to find value-judgments (approval of Athenian democracy, belief in its importance and contemporary relevance, defence of it against some modern criticisms) in some passages in *The Athenian Assembly*, and objected to 'H.'s converging assumptions that Athenian democracy is best understood as a "constitution", and that we can best understand this constitution, and the principles on which it was based, by analyzing the relations between formal institutions of government'; 'H.'s argument is likely to convince those who are used to thinking of good scholarship as objective and without ideological bias, and of "the evidence" as transparent, neutral, and authoritative. ... But if both the texts and the a priori assumptions employed by scholars are *social and* ideological constructs, the issues of authority and meaning become much more complex.'

43

Hansen replied in an article 'On the Importance of Institutions in an Analysis of Athenian Democracy':[44] the current preference for focusing on interest groups and their activities (which may be represented as political syntax or physiology) rather than on formal institutions and their working (political morphology or anatomy) is appropriate to states in which informal activity is more important than formal machinery, but the Athenian democracy was at the institutional end of the spectrum of political systems, so that (whatever may be the case for other systems) a study of the institutions is fundamental to an understanding of how Athenian democracy worked. Hansen did not respond to the charge that his scholarship is not objective but is an ideological construct. We shall have to return to this confrontation.

Politics and politicians

In the early twentieth century Roman historians reacting against the study of *Staatsaltertümer* had turned from institutions to the study of politics and politicians. M. Gelzer published *Die Nobilität der römischen Republik* ('The Nobility of the Roman Republic') in 1912 and an article on 'Die Nobilität der Kaiserzeit' ('The Nobility of the Imperial Period') shortly afterwards; F. Münzer published *Römische Adelsparteien und Adelsfamilien* in 1920;[45] and the 'prosopographical' approach to Roman politicians and their connections reached the English-speaking world in R. Syme's *The Roman Revolution* of 1939, and remained influential for the next half-century. For Syme, at any rate, this was not just an alternative to an outworn approach but had contemporary relevance: Syme claimed that his 'deliberately critical attitude towards Augustus' and 'rather lenient' treatment of others reflected the Republican sentiments of the principal Roman historians (p. vii); but his view that 'in all ages, whatever the form and name of government, ... an oligarchy lurks behind the façade' (p. 7) echoes the 'iron law of oligarchy' propounded with reference to the modern world by R. Michels in 1911;[46] and his hostile view of the often-admired Augustus reads as if it was conditioned by his response to the fascist leaders of Europe in the 1930s.[47]

This approach was then emulated in Athenian history, in particular by R. Sealey in several articles in the 1950s and 1960s.[48] J.K. Davies in *Athenian Propertied Families, 600-300 BC*[49] assembled the data on which a history of the Athenian upper class could be written; the general discussion of the data which had occupied the introductory volume of Davies' Oxford thesis was revised as *Wealth and the Power of Wealth in Classical Athens* in 1981 – though by then he felt obliged to label it 'pre-theoretical'.[50] In 1971 W.R. Connor published *The New Politicians of Fifth-Century Athens*, in which he attributed to A.F. Bentley's *The Process of Government* of 1908 the principle that 'the study of political groups is the best way to understand how the government of a state operates';[51] another exponent of the prosopographical approach to Athenian history was P.J. Bicknell.[52]

A constant theme in Sealey's work is that scholars have greatly overestimated the Athenians' interest in and desire for democracy: for instance, the reform of the Areopagus in 462/1, which some see as a conscious attempt to make Athens more democratic,[53] he argues was simply an improvement in accounting procedures[54] – and E. Ruschenbusch has suggested that if there was an ulterior purpose it was to make it easier for Ephialtes and his supporters to change Athens' foreign policy.[55] In a more recent book Sealey has argued that what the Athenians finally achieved by the fourth century was not *demokratia* but the rule of law.[56] Here we have the ultimate in anti-ideology, a claim that the Athenians themselves never had an ideological interest in democracy.[57]

Exploitation

The original opposition to Grote's championing of democracy, which lingered to the early twentieth century, came from conservatives who objected that Athens gave power to lower-class men who were not worthy of it. But it is also possible to object to Athenian democracy on the liberal grounds that the *demos* was a restricted body of adult male citizens who exploited others – slaves, women and the inhabitants of the other states in Athens' fifth-century empire.

In the modern world objections to slavery began to be voiced in the seventeenth century and gathered pace in the eighteenth; at the time of American independence the northern states, which had comparatively few slaves, were prepared to renounce slavery but the southern were not; at different dates within the nineteenth century the countries of the world banned first the international trading of slaves and then slavery within their own borders.[58] At the end of the eighteenth century the independent United States and the French Revolution began a movement towards extending basic political rights (and, in particular, the right to vote in elections) to all

adult male citizens, without imposing property or other quali-
fications; that continued in the nineteenth century, and it was
followed by pressure to extend equal rights to women, which
was achieved in many countries in the course of the twentieth
century.[59] American independence also marked the beginning
of the end of the European states' overseas empires: the United
Kingdom granted the near-independence of 'dominion' status
to colonies populated largely by settlers from Britain, beginning with Canada in 1867;[60] colonies in which a minority of
European settlers had governed a majority indigenous population achieved independence in the second half of the twentieth
century.[61]

The legacy of the past is still with us. Descendants of slaves
form a substantial proportion of the population of the United
States and some other countries; there are some countries
where women have still not achieved formal equality, and
many where they and other groups (such as recent immigrants)
complain that they are disadvantaged in practice; former
colonies labour under difficulties for which they blame their
former rulers, and the former rulers find it hard to be helpful
without being interfering. From today's viewpoint, it is all too
easy to see democratic Athens as an exploiting state.

Slavery and the position of women in antiquity were in the
generation of Grote handled charitably,[62] while in the southern United States in the middle of the nineteenth century the
Greeks and Romans were enlisted in support of slavery;[63] but
by the late nineteenth century there was beginning a reaction
against slavery and the treatment of women in the ancient
world, and so less indulgence was shown by such writers as
A.C. Bradley and A.J. Grant.[64] In the twentieth century mat-

ters of this kind were among those dealt with by A.E. Zimmern in *The Greek Commonwealth*: he examined the Athenians' record on slaves and on women, giving Athens a clean bill of health on slaves (5th ed., p. 395) and on women trying to do so but admitting that in the end he could not (pp. 333-42). As for the Athenian empire, in a chapter entitled 'The Development of Citizenship: Liberty, or the Rule of Empire', Zimmern painted a glowing picture of beneficent centralisation in which

> The process was so gradual, and the control so wisely exercised, that the allies could not easily put their hand on any particular cause of complaint. There was plenty of grumbling. ... But of practical grievances we hear little or nothing.[65]

J.C. Stobart in *The Glory that was Greece* set the 'cruel toil' of the slaves against 'this brilliant society' (p. 145), but it was left to R.J. Hopper, revising the book in 1964, to add exploitation of the empire to exploitation of the slaves (4th ed., p. 139). A.W. Gomme wrote a heterodox article on women, attacking the standard view that they enjoyed considerable freedom in the Homeric world but little in classical Athens.[66]

We have seen that public profession of ideology is characteristic of Marxists. A fundamental theme of Marxism is the exploitation, economically and in other respects, of a disadvantaged class by an advantaged.[67] In the USSR it was the standard view that Athens was an exploiting society. Two Soviet textbooks which have been translated into western languages are Korovkin, *History of the Ancient World* (for young pupils in schools), who analysed the whole ancient world in terms of a class struggle in which the slaves were at war against their owners, and mentioned Athens' treatment of women, metics and the empire but without emphasis; and a more advanced book, Diakov & Kovalev (edd.), *Histoire de l'antiquité*, where Athens' democracy is repeatedly labelled a slave-based democracy, F. Engels is quoted in support of the view that it did at least mark an improvement on archaic aristocracy and oriental despotism, but the reader is then warned not to rate it too highly (p. 397).

'As imperialist fantasies migrated from England to the United States, British pride began to give way to American squeamishness',[68] and as Marxism became influential among western academics there developed a line of thought in which Athenian male citizens' exploitation of women, slaves and imperial subjects was brought increasingly into the foreground and made the basis for a hostile view of democratic Athens. 'By the standards of the late twentieth century, the Athenians were not very nice people.'[69]

M.I. Finley, who began his life and his career in the United States but became politically suspect in the McCarthy era and migrated to the United Kingdom,[70] was one of the first to adopt a strongly critical position.[71] In an article asking 'Was Greek Civilization Based on Slave Labour?' he argued that 'the cities in which individual freedom reached its highest expression – most obviously Athens – were cities in which chattel slavery flourished. ... One aspect of Greek history, in short, is the advance, hand in hand, of freedom and slavery.'[72] In an attempt to draw up a 'balance-sheet' for the fifth-century Athenian empire he deplored asking 'whether Athens "exploited her allies in any extensive way" ' but concluded that

'Athenian imperialism employed all the forms of material exploitation that were available and possible in that society'.[73] But, although Finley was not disposed to gloss over the Athenians' exploitation of slaves and of their empire, he was a believer in democracy, and in the relevance of Athenian democracy to the modern world. In *Democracy, Ancient and Modern*[74] he insisted that 'the system worked, insofar as that is a useful judgment about any form of government'. Direct application of Athenian practice to the modern world was not to be contemplated, but the political education of the citizens, the political involvement of the citizens and the responsibility of the citizens in the use of their power were features to be preferred to the ignorance and apathy of a modern democracy run by a political élite.[75] The empire was a necessary condition for the creation of the Athenian democracy, but on the fall of the empire at the end of the fifth century 'the system was so deeply entrenched that no one dared attempt to replace it' (p. [1]49 = [2]87). Similarly in *Politics in the Ancient World* he was happy to use the word 'democracy' and to give the Greeks and Romans the credit for inventing politics and the public discussion of and decision on political issues; but he began with a chapter in which he insisted that 'The choice of those who govern and the ways in which they govern depend on the structure of the particular society under examination. A central feature of the societies with which we are concerned was the important presence of slaves; another was the severe restriction among the Greeks of access to citizenship; a third was the exclusion of women from any direct participation in political or governmental activity.'[76]

To take a few more examples, R.A. Padgug represented the

democratic *polis* as the 'new commune' which resulted from attacks on the 'old commune' of the aristocratic *polis*, dependent on its exploitation of non-members, but condemned by the insufficiency of resources to disintegrate in a struggle between rich and poor.[77] O. Patterson (himself descended from slaves), in *Freedom*, i,[78] points out that democracy survived the end of the empire (p. 97), but stresses the importance of slaves, metics and women for the freedom of the male citizens: 'The high point of the democracy [he makes Pericles' introduction of jury pay coincide with his citizenship law in 451/0] was also the high point of its exclusiveness'. More idiosyncratically, the journalist I.F. Stone, who turned in retirement to the history of freedom of thought, approached the trial and condemnation of Socrates with the assumption that 'it was a black mark for Athens and the freedom it symbolized'. But he wanted 'to give the Athenian side of the story, to mitigate the city's crime and thereby remove some of the stigma the trial left on democracy and Athens', and so in *The Trial of Socrates*[79] he represented Socrates as an authoritarian élitist who was fundamentally hostile to the values of the egalitarian Athenians: i.e. the execution of Socrates was wrong, but if anybody deserved to be executed for his opinions Socrates did.

Recently, however, V.D. Hanson, while not denying the sinfulness of the sins which it is fashionable to focus on, has pointed out (correctly) that

By and large, the sins of the Greeks – slavery, sexism, economic exploitation, ethnic chauvinism – are largely the sins of man common to *all* cultures at *all* times. The 'others' in the Greek world – foreigners, slaves, women – were also 'others' in *all* other societies of the time.[80]

In Britain a more positive view tended for a time to persist. W.G. Forrest in *The Emergence of Greek Democracy*[81] mentioned the empire but more emphatically the glories of Athens, stressed that the oligarchs of the late fifth century behaved much more badly than the 'ordinary Athenians', and rejected a view of Athens divided between mob and élite. G.E.M. de Ste Croix, in *The Class Struggle in the Ancient Greek World*, set out to write 'the first book ... which begins by explaining the central features of Marx's historical method and defining the concepts and categories involved, and then proceeds to demonstrate how these instruments of analysis may be used in practice to explain the main events, processes, institutions and ideas that prevailed at various times over a long period of history' (p. ix). He seems to have regarded himself as the master's one true disciple, complaining not only of 'the extreme ignorance of Marx's thought which prevails throughout most of the west' (p. x) but also of 'the disastrous developments of Marx's thought by many of his followers' (p. xi), and insisting that 'the meaning [de Ste Croix attaches] to the expression "class struggle" represents the fundamental thought of Marx himself' (p. 3). He wrote approvingly of Athenian democracy and believed that 'the political class struggle at Athens was on the whole very muted in the [classical] period' (p. 290), acknowledged without stressing it the limitation of citizenship to adult male Athenians, claimed that the empire was unique 'in that the ruling city relied very much on the support of the lower classes in the subject states' (p.

290), and contrasted this brief period of virtue with 'the gradual extinction of Greek democracy' (p. 300) from the fourth century onwards.[82] D. Stockton has written an enthusiastic account of *The Classical Athenian Democracy*,[83] remarking in a final footnote on Athens' treatment of women and slaves that 'to make too much of either issue is to be guilty of anachronism'.

Recently, however, there has been squeamishness in Britain too. Osborne has remarked that 'Athenian democracy went part and parcel with an Athenian way of life which we would judge illiberal, culturally chauvinist and narrowly restrictive. It was, essentially, the product of a closed society.'[84] (However, in his Cambridge inaugural lecture, delivered in 2002 on the fiftieth anniversary of A.H.M. Jones' Cambridge inaugural lecture, his concern was not to pass judgment on Athenian democracy but to show how the study of it was changed by Jones and has been further changed since, and to insist on the importance of 'joined-up writing', in which the results of different kinds of investigation are integrated.[85]) P. Cartledge has insisted on the relevance of Athenian democracy to our own concerns and on what by present-day criteria are the vices as well as the virtues of Athenian democracy;[86] and M. Beard in a review of a book on Roman republican politics has complained of excessive adulation of Athenian democracy by leftward-leaning scholars and stressed that it was the Romans who made voting by secret ballot the norm for decision-making assemblies and who extended citizenship to liberated slaves.[87]

5

Athenian Democracy and Us

America and the European tradition

Americans seem to have developed a particularly self-conscious relationship with the ancient world. We have seen that the Founding Fathers of the United States did not derive their views from ancient history but were happy to cite ancient history in support of their views. There was a division between those who thought that a European classical education was all the more important for Europeans settled as colonists in a new world and those who thought it was irrelevant to them.[1] However, with the development of professional scholarship in the nineteenth century American scholars aligned themselves firmly with European concerns and standards of scholarship, and the range which they embraced included, and has continued to include, classical scholarship: two particularly important figures were E. Everett, who in 1815 at the age of twenty-two was appointed as the first Eliot Professor of Greek Literature at Harvard, who obtained a Ph.D. from Göttingen in 1817;[2] and, in the next generation, B.L. Gildersleeve, who studied in Germany for three years in the 1850s, and after service in the University of Virginia (and in the American Civil War) became founding Professor of Greek at Johns Hopkins

University in 1876 and founding editor of the *American Journal of Philology* in 1880.[3] This attachment of the Americans to the classics and their determination to anchor themselves in the European tradition has had some remarkable results: in particular J.H. Finley, Sr., while President of the City College, New York, between 1909 and 1913, introduced the practice by which the College's students on graduating swore the oath of the Athenian ephebes (young men who between the ages of eighteen and twenty underwent a programme of patriotic and military training) in Finley's translation – a practice which continues in that college and has spread to a great many educational institutions and organisations of other kinds in the United States.[4]

Recently, however, there have been further developments. A rift has opened between those who still champion this anchoring of American education in the European tradition[5] and relativists who object to concentration on the deeds and writings of 'dead white European males' and insist that all activities and all levels of culture, among all peoples, are of equal validity – or, indeed, that the works of people other than dead white European males are positively to be preferred.[6] Americans who continue to study Greece and Rome have had to fight harder to demonstrate that the subject is still worth studying; and a new insistence on relevance has not only coloured the studies of Athenian democracy with which I am concerned in this book but has led, for instance, to the attempt in M. Bernal's *Black Athena* to find black African origins for Greek culture.[7]

America has also been the driving-force for a kind of globalisation and commercialisation whose effects can be seen not only in such matters as the styles of casual clothing increasingly worn all over the world but also in scholarship, and especially in works published in the English language.[8] The publications of academics have for a long time covered a range, from highly specialised works addressed by academics to their fellow-academics, via works intended for advanced students in universities or more elementary students in schools, to works intended for interested members of the general public – which serve both as evangelism for the subject and as a demonstration that what academics do is not of concern only to a few eccentrics and is not undeserving of public support. Those whose first language is one of the world's minority languages tend to make a sharp division, using one of the major languages for their specialised works, addressed to specialists around the world who may not be able to read the minority language, but their own language for works of evangelism, addressed to fellow-citizens in their own countries, and sometimes in these works dealing with local concerns which are of less interest to the wider world.[9] But nowadays it seems that publishers, even University Presses, are driven more by accountants and less by professors than in the past. A book which may sell tens of copies a year to academics, and may continue to do so for decades, is not considered to be viable: a successful book is one which sells well, and in a few years is sold out, leaving room in the warehouse for newer books. Few publishers would now be happy with a book like W.S. Ferguson's *The Treasurers of Athena*, of 1932, which unashamedly began its preface, 'This is a work for specialists'.[10] Nowadays pills have to be concealed in jam, and even works of serious scholarship – which of course are still written and published – have to be made accessible, for instance with all quotations in ancient and modern languages translated into English,[11] and relevant, with a message for today's readers. Sometimes those who write works of serious scholarship try to appease their publishers with an eye-catching title and a contemporary message added to the beginning and the end; sometimes publishers try to suggest that a book is more populist than it actually is.[12]

Indeed, scholars are expected to write for Winnie-the-Pooh.[13] The comments of an American assessor on the formal proposal for another book which I am to write included: 'This textbook will be most accessible to today's students if it is written in a fairly informal style – adopting a conversational tone, avoiding long sentences and difficult vocabulary (by students' standards – e.g. most of my students do not know the meaning of "hegemony")'; and the editor of a book to which I am contributing a chapter has asked me, for the sake of American undergraduate readers, to shorten my longer sentences and to remove the expressions *amour propre* and *force majeure*.[14] The effect has been less marked on articles in periodicals, though even there editors urge authors to cater for monoglot readers; but in books, particularly in the English language, and most particularly in the United States, there is a striking difference between what is put out by academic publishers now and what was put out half a century ago.[15] A book which can be recommended to American undergraduates will sell far more copies than a book addressed to professors; and, confident in the accessibility to all of the English language and in the relevance to all of American concerns, the publishers will market the book world-wide.

It is against this background that we must see the most recent American work on Athenian democracy. 'The Athenians were not very nice people'[16] was a concession made by some scholars to those who wanted to dethrone the Greeks and Romans, as in the second half of the twentieth century Americans became increasingly uncomfortable with the treatment by Athens' adult male citizens of non-citizens both inside the city and in their fifth-century empire. More recently there has in some quarters been a reaction against that discomfiture, or at any rate a tendency to place other considerations on the other side of the balance. The most glowing account of the fifth-century empire was written by M.F. McGregor, a Briton who moved to North America in his childhood; and J.L. Cargill has argued that the Second Athenian League of the fourth century was better at keeping its virtuous foundation promises than has generally been believed.[17] McGregor's book is particularly striking. In the final chapter, 'Empire: A Verdict',[18] we read:

We shall be wise to bear in mind that since the Second World War the very words 'empire' and 'imperialism' have acquired unpleasant connotations. ... The historian's duty, on the other hand, is to gather and analyse the evidence, dispassionately; only then will he express a judgement. [p. 166] ... The charges levelled against the Athenians ... create a misleading impression. ... The truth is that no single imperial practice could be judged gravely oppressive, irritating in individual cases though it might be. [p. 174] ... [The allies] wanted freedom at any price [pp. 174-5] ... [but] the Athenians resolved that peace and safety brought greater blessings than sovereignty. [p. 177]

A strange attempt to acknowledge criticisms of the internal state of Athens but to find a way of compensating for them is made in a recent book by N.F. Jones, *The Associations of Classical Athens* – subtitled *The Response to Democracy*. Much of the book is devoted to the detailed study of various sub-groups within Athens (demes and tribes; phratries; 'voluntary associations' such as *hetaireiai* and *gene*), but behind that there is an acknowledged political agenda. In his concluding chapter Jones writes:

It is obvious that the democratic government fell short of meeting what we know or may reasonably suppose to have been the expectations of both the citizen and non-citizen populations. To be sure, the nature of the problem would be conceptualized differently according to the rank, socioeconomic situation, and general predicament of the particular Athenian resident or group. [Aristocrats would feel deprived of their birthright; special-interest groups would find themselves outnumbered; public-spirited citizens would be frustrated by Athens' complex participatory system.] The *de iure* disfranchised, women of the citizen class, metics, and even those slaves who had enjoyed citizen status in their place of origin must have found exceedingly arbitrary a regime that automatically excluded themselves while, equally automatically, bestowing the mantle of privilege upon all males of the citizen class meeting the minimal twin requirements of majority and legitimate birth. [p. 289]

The purpose of his book is to demonstrate that the sub-groups provided opportunities for activity and satisfaction to members of the Athenian population who were unable to achieve activity and satisfaction through the major institutions of the *polis* itself. There is of course a degree of truth in that, as there is for any state which is of more than minimal size and has a variety of sub-groups within it. However, in my judgment he goes much further than the evidence justifies in arguing that the sub-groups tended gradually to overlook the *polis*' boundaries between citizens and non-citizens; and what he 'may reasonably suppose' to have been the expectations of non-citizens may seem reasonable to a modern American but surely did not in a world in which exclusion from citizenship not only of women and of slaves but even of free men who were not of citizen ancestry was not peculiar to Athens but was entirely normal.

J. Ober has been one of a group of American scholars who are much concerned with the contemporary relevance of Athenian democracy and who object to scholars who do not show a similar concern.[19] In the review article on M.H. Hansen which I have mentioned above he writes, 'One must ask not only whether his conclusions correctly answer the questions he has posed, but whether he has posed meaningful questions (i.e., questions with heuristic value for readers) in meaningful terms (i.e., terms that are readily understood by readers and accurately describe ancient political and social structures).'[20] His *Mass and Elite in Democratic Athens* begins with a section

60

on 'Democracy: Athenian and Modern' (pp. 3-10 ch. i.A): he contrasts Athenian democracy with the modern democracy by governing élite, and regards as an over-statement the view that 'the success of the democracy ... rested largely on its insistence on a marked distinction between citizens (whatever their social status) on the one hand, and all categories of noncitizens on the other'.[21] He insists that to deny the name democracy to Athens because of its exclusion of Others is ahistorical, condemns those who have over-stressed the similarities between ancient and modern democracy (and who have, for instance, looked for political parties of the modern kind in Athens) but insists that to over-stress the differences would lead to sterile antiquarianism, and declares as his objective to 'make the Athenian democracy look both explicable in its own terms and an accessible tool for political analysis and action by those who are, or would be, citizens of democratic states' (p. 9). He cites as a prominent holder of the élitist view of democracy Michels, whose 'iron law' that in any organisation an oligarchy is bound to develop has been mentioned above; and his own thesis is that in the Athenian democracy an oligarchy did not develop but the Athenians managed to combine economic and social inequality with political equality through the 'ideological hegemony of the masses',[22] by which the members of the élite who claimed a leading position in Athens had perpetually to justify themselves to the *demos* as acting not in their own interest but in that of the *demos*.

Americans were particularly enthusiastic in making the 2,500th anniversary of the reforms of Cleisthenes (508/7), in 1993/4, an occasion for celebrating 2,500 years of democracy: in this connection the National Endowment for the Humanities funded projects directed by Ober and C.W. Hedrick, and by Hedrick and J.P. Euben.[23] Ober in his Introductory Remarks in an exhibition catalogue conceded, 'There is much that the modern democrat is likely to find repugnant about ancient Athens' (the exhibition included two sections on 'The Unenfranchised: I. Women / II. Slaves and Resident Aliens');

> But we would be indulging in absurdly anachronistic complacency if we were to refuse to learn from the Athenian experience of democracy on the grounds that their value system is at odds with that of the modern Western world. ... Despite the ... doubts [of the Constitutional Framers of the United States], Athenian Demokratia seems in some ways quite similar to modern American conceptions of government. Yet in other ways the Athenian approach to democratic government was surprisingly different from any modern political régime. Assessing the similarities and differences between ancient and modern democratic practices and ideals can help today's citizens sharpen their own definition of what democracy now is – and what they believe it should become.

In Britain this anniversary prompted a book edited by J. Dunn, *Democracy: The Unfinished Journey, 508 BC to AD 1993*.[24] Dunn himself stressed the importance of freedom both for the individual and for the community of citizens; I quote some passages from his concluding chapter:

5. Athenian Democracy and Us

What ended democracy in Athens ... was ... the military power of the kingdom of Macedon, and what ended independent democratic rule throughout the Mediterranean world over the next two centuries was the far greater and more enduring military power of Rome. [p. 244] ... Representative democracy is democracy made safe for the modern state. ... To an Athenian eye this version of democracy would seem not so much tamed ... as *neutered*. ... But this is a little too brisk, since representative democracy has proved with some pertinacity to be well able to combine the practical viability of a relatively coherent system of political authority (a modern state) with the more insinuating appeals of the idea of popular self-rule. To its critics, this deftly synthetic capacity has always seemed a monstrous conjuring trick. [pp. 248-9] ... A cynical view of the history of democracy would see in the term's verbal triumph a mere mirage, a comprehensive and potentially hazardous condition of mass delusion. But that does not make it true. What does it leave out? It is clear that what has survived from the experience of ancient democracy is not simply a word, but also a diffuse and urgent hope. [p. 256][25]

C. Farrar, an American who wrote a Ph.D. thesis at the British Cambridge, wrote on *The Origins of Democratic Thinking*:[26] she sought to rebut those who 'have characterized the triumphant practice of direct, participating democracy at Athens as mob rule, or as the hollow creation of a slave-owning elite or, at best, as admirable but outmoded' (p. 1), and she found particularly in Thucydides and praised as democratic the idea of a régime based on 'autonomous participation ... under the tutelage of reason ... guided by an elite in the interests of the whole' (p. 267). The dependence of the democracy on women, slaves and the empire was mentioned but not stressed (p. 8). And this is another study which claims relevance to our world: Athenian democracy 'has *force* for us because it poses a genuine and challenging alternative to current modes of life and thought. And it has force for *us* because it can be seen to have been the response to conditions importantly analogous to those that have fostered our own unease' (p. 14). She concludes:

> We have lost confidence in politics, in the possibility of reconciling the autonomy of particular individuals with a social order that can withstand reflective scrutiny. ...We rest discontent with a schism between the realms of the 'private' and the 'public' citizen. ... It is democracy, as conceived and lived by Athenians in the fifth century BC, that offers at least the possibility of healing this spiritual and social fragmentation. [p. 274] ... Greater democracy does not, therefore, mean the deployment of such mechanisms as a computerized voting procedure, but rather the creation of forms of political participation, education and integration suited to modern society. [p. 277]

Ober in a review article on that book, R.K. Sinclair, *Democracy and Participation*, and E.M. Wood, *Peasant-Citizen and Slave*, objects to Farrar's choice of texts through which to investigate democracy and complains that the dispensation which she championed would not have been regarded as democratic either by the Greeks in general or by the authors on whom she based it; he regards Sinclair's book as a good introduction to recent scholarship but finds it too institutional for his taste; he is attracted by Wood's view that Athens owed its democratic ethos to its peasant-citizens, who were not parasitic on slave labour but were hard-working men, but regrets that 'much of her argument remains to be proved, and some of Wood's positions may not stand up to detailed philological scrutiny'.[27]

A number of books have been published recently in America on The Athenians and Us. *Athenian Political Thought and the Reconstruction of American Democracy*[28] deplores a tendency to champion in the name of democracy the leadership of a passive *demos* by 'responsible elites', laments that conservatives have taken over the hostility to democracy of Plato and Aristotle, and suggests that thanks to new evidence and new approaches the modern study of Athenian democracy can speak to modern America as earlier study could not, and may help today's society to educate itself for active democracy. Several contributors stress the exclusive nature of the citizen *demos*, but B.S. Strauss draws attention to the greater willingness of Athens to absorb immigrants in the sixth century than in the classical period; there are chapters by S.S. Monoson and Euben in which they try to rescue Plato for democracy;[29] S.S. Wolin and E.M. Wood contrast the revolutionary and truly democratic nature of Athenian people-power with modern, representative-democratic constitutions; J.R. Wallach claims that classical Athens had, and modern America needs, an understanding of virtue which is compatible with the principle of democracy.

Another book with chapters by many of the same contributors is *Demokratia: A Conversation on Democracies, Ancient and Modern*,[30] which originated in a conference held in Washington, DC, in 1993 in connection with the celebration of 2,500 years organised by Ober and Hedrick. In their Introduction the editors refer to the project, whose origin they attribute to Finley in his *Democracy, Ancient and Modern*, 'of applying insights gained from political and social theory to problems in Greek history, and in turn using the Greek historical experience of democracy as a resource for building normative political theory'. The modern world can usually be detected in the background, but there is more discussion of Greece for its own sake and less explicit engagement with the modern world in this book than in that mentioned in the previous paragraph. Among the contributors most openly concerned with the modern world, Euben continues his attempt to establish a democratic Plato (and is here answered by B.R. Barber); Wood, looking at the *banausoi* (lower-class workers), again contrasts classical Athens favourably with modern representative democracies. M. Ostwald contrasts the Greek view of a citizen as one who shares in the community with the American view of a citizen as one who has rights which not even the state may infringe; while R.W. Wallace notes that an Athenian's freedoms were less secure than an American's in theory, because there was no Bill of Rights to protect them against the state, but as secure in practice, because the Athenian state did not in fact interfere with the citizens' freedoms unnecessarily. Hansen (to whose chapter Wood's is a response) argues that the modern concept of liberty is similar to, though not derived from, the Athenian.[31] P.B. Manville, a classicist who has moved to work in the commercial world, gives the book a startling conclusion in a chapter which compares democratic Athens not with the modern state but with the modern knowledge-based profit-making or non-profit-making organisation, which expects its members to be enthusiastic and involved participants rather than employees who know their place and obey orders.

A book by a single author which tries to invoke Athens in connection with present-day America is E. Sagan's *The Honey and the Hemlock: Democracy and Paranoia in Ancient Athens and Modern America*. He states forcefully the contrast between 'the ideal and the reality of a democratic polity based on a complex and moral conception of citizenship' and Athens' behaviour to its subjects and wartime opponents and to the slaves and women in its midst, claiming that 'it is of crucial importance to try to understand what gross immoralities are still compatible with the forms of democratic society. Athens provides us with one of the sharpest examples, if not the sharpest, of this awesome human contradiction' (p. 2). However, 'if, because of [the] exclusions [of non-citizens] we would deny the name "democracy" to such a society, then we must be consistent and do the same to the state established in North America in 1789' (p. 7). Unlike Ober, he believes that inequalities in wealth and capacity for leadership 'lead to the creation of a political elite that rules even where the *demos* retains sovereignty' (p. 274). His essential message is that democracy is possible when we banish paranoia sufficiently to trust one another and to accept the concept of a loyal opposition – and no society, either in the ancient world or in the modern, has yet come near to banishing that paranoia totally.

Ober has collected a number of his papers and reviews in a volume entitled *The Athenian Revolution*.[32] The modern interest which he professes there is in political theory rather than in the practices of the present-day United States (e.g. p. 3); he also professes concern with the history of ideologies, and a desire to find a sane middle way between positivist attempts to achieve 'an impossible level of objectivity' and 'reader-response' approaches which find in any object of study what they have determined in advance to find (pp. 8-9). Several chapters employ the view of Athenian democracy which he expounded in *Mass and Elite*. Additionally, he frequently makes use of the concept of 'speech-acts' introduced to philosophy by J.L. Austin.[33] There had been a tendency in linguistic philosophy in the mid twentieth century to focus on statements, which after an appropriate procedure of verification could be judged true or false, and A.J. Ayer had maintained that 'metaphysical' statements in such areas as morality or religion are incapable of verification and are therefore not the statements they purport to be but simply expressions of emotion.[34] Austin, to broaden the scope of this kind of philosophy, drew attention to utterances such as 'I do' in a marriage ceremony, which are not statements, which may or may not be true, but 'performative utterances', which are an integral part of an act such as marrying, and which may or may not be 'felicitous', i.e. correctly and successfully performed. Ober applies this concept to, for instance, 'Resolved by (the council and) the people', the enactment formula[35] of an Athenian decree, which can be categorised not as a statement of fact but as the performative utterance by which the Athenians enacted the decree.[36] In the final chapter of the book, a paper which he was invited to write on the *polis* as a society,[37] he asks how Athenian democracy measures up against an ancient and a modern ideal – the 'best possible *polis*' of Aristotle, *Politics* VII, which unlike democratic Athens excluded ordinary working men from citizenship (N.B. *Politics* VII.1328b33-1329a2, 1329a17-26), and the 'well-ordered' society of J. Rawls, which attempts to ground satisfactory provision for all its members in an agreed conception of justice and a 'difference principle' to mitigate inequalities by favouring the disadvantaged.[38] Ober judges that by Rawls' standards the citizen community of Athens did well, and indeed better than many other societies, but the whole community of people living in Athens did not.

6

How to Study Athenian Democracy

Making the past meaningful

There is nothing new in the colouring of the study of Athenian democracy by the student's own political views, or in the notion that such study may have relevance for the world in which the student lives; nor is there anything new in disagreement resulting from the different views of different students: the opposition to democracy of Mitford, and the different hostile reactions to him of Macaulay and of Grote, provide one clear example. After the late nineteenth and early twentieth centuries, when it was fashionable for scholars to profess, if not to achieve, scientific objectivity, in the mid twentieth century open ideological commitment returned with Marxism, and in the late twentieth century the search for authoritative answers gave way to the babel of post-modernism. Today in the study of Athenian democracy, as in ancient history more generally, there is a range from scholars who in their own eyes if not in their critics' keep the effect of their ideology on their scholarship to a minimum, to those who are ideologically committed and proud of it; from those who seek correct answers to factual questions, to those who seek to penetrate the *mentalité* of the actors in the drama; from those whose notion of relevance is that history makes us aware of problems and of possible responses to them, and helps us to understand how we have arrived where we are now, to those who seek in the past definite models and lessons for the present; from those who believe that we cannot make of history whatever we like, to those who think that we cannot do anything but make of history whatever we like.

I am one of the historians manoeuvring within those ranges: although in an earlier chapter I wrote of myself in the third person, I cannot be impartial, and I shall here use the first person. I am not myself conscious of having an agenda in the modern world which colours my study of the ancient, but I realise that some will allege that I cannot fail to have one and that I am the worse for not acknowledging it. In the study of the ancient world, I try to understand those whose positions are different from my own, and their reasons for adopting those positions, but I have my own positions, and although I am a pluralist I am not a relativist.[1] As I indicated above, in Chapter 1, I believe that there is value in different approaches to history, but I do not believe that any approach which anybody may choose to adopt is necessarily of equal validity. We cannot alter what happened in the past; it is our duty as historians, as far as we can, to discover what happened in the past, and to interpret it in ways which not only make it meaningful for us but also do justice to it; and those who in their determination to make the past meaningful fail to do justice to it are failing as historians.

It is, of course, easier to proclaim the principle than to apply it, since we tend to persuade ourselves that in making the past meaningful we are indeed doing justice to it, and not many will expose the unreasonableness of their 'reasonable expectations' as blatantly as N.F. Jones in his study of Associations.[2] Because Ober has articulated his views in detail, I return to his comments on other students of Athenian democracy.

I agree with Ober in opposing an extreme naïve positivism which thinks it sufficient to 'discover the "objective truth" about the past by "letting the sources speak for themselves" '[3] and believes in an antiquarian spirit that 'discovering the truth about the past' is a sufficient and indeed the only justification for studying history – though I am not sure that anybody now active in the field actually holds such a position.[4] I believe that the study of history is useful, at least in the austere sense that it enlarges our understanding of human life by allowing us to see how and with what results people have confronted situations, ideas and problems which 'in accordance with human nature are likely to occur in the same or similar form some time again',[5] and to see how situations, ideas and problems current in our own time have come about. Those of us who are committed professionally to its study rely for funding and more general support on people and institutions who are not likewise committed; at the level of detail we are likely enough to engage in 'intra-disciplinary debates over questions that are of primary significance within our paradigm, but meaningless to anyone outside the field';[6] but we need to convince the wider world that the results of our investigations and our intra-disciplinary debates will produce something of value to more than our fellow-specialists.

Ober makes a much stronger claim for the usefulness of history:[7]

6. How to Study Athenian Democracy

A historiographical model or historiographic product should represent some aspect of the past in a way that is meaningful and useful. [p. 135 = 15] ... A model or historiographic product is (in my formulation) 'meaningful' to the extent that it *makes sense to readers and* has heuristic value *for them*:[8] that is to say, to the extent that it helps people to act in 'the real world' and to assess for themselves the significance of their own and others' actions, by viewing those actions against a broader context. [p. 136 = 16] Historical paradigm formulation, by its nature, inevitably entails emphasizing the importance of certain categories of past social activity and cultural products, while obscuring others. ... Categories of activity and cultural products relegated to the sidelines by the dominant paradigm may not disappear from view, but are necessarily made to appear insignificant. [p. 136 = 17]

Ober is committed to scholarship as well as to relevance, and he states also that

Professional historians ... feel that they have a proprietary disciplinary interest in controlling interpretations of the past; and ... have a rational desire, based at least in part on self-interest, in seeing that the interpretations of the past used by (for example) politicians are based on the highest possible standards of honesty and rigor. [p. 136 = 16]

But he has ventured into dangerous territory. We have seen that he is attracted by E.M. Wood's picture of an Athenian democracy which derived its character from the peasant-citizens on whom it was based, but in that instance he draws back from the brink in fear that her case may not be sufficiently grounded in a proper study of the sources.[9]

In his criticism of M.H. Hansen[10] he claims that

A monograph or article by Hansen, like any other text, is best understood as an ideological construct.[11] ... One must ask ... also whether he has posed meaningful questions *(i.e., questions with heuristic value for readers)*[12] in meaningful terms (i.e., in terms that are readily understood by readers and accurately describe ancient political and social structures). [p. 323 = 110] ... Is political power in Athens best conceptualized as legal sovereignty? [p. 324 = 111] ... Hansen ... generally subordinates sociopolitical questions to institutional concerns. [p. 326 = 113] ... The primary principle involved in democratic decision making at Athens was not separation of institutional powers, but demotic control of the public realm. [p. 331 = 119]

Now it is clear that Ober wants a picture of democratic Athens which is different from Hansen's, but on what level is Ober disagreeing with Hansen? Is it that Hansen 'does not accurately describe ancient political and social structures', that he is objectively wrong and Ober objectively right in characterising the democracy? Is it that each is right within his own terms of reference but that Ober has more appropriate terms of reference because with regard to the concerns of today's world Ober is 'posing meaningful questions in meaningful terms', which will be 'readily understood by readers', but Hansen is not? Or should we after all embrace a thorough relativism and say that Hansen's investigations are based on his chosen 'social or ideological construct', Ober's are based on his construct and any number of constructs may be equally valid? Is Ober claiming that Hansen's approach fails, and his own succeeds, in doing justice to Athenian democracy? or in making Athenian democracy meaningful to our world? or simply in matching Ober's preferences? Hansen in his reply,[13] as one would expect from some of Ober's criticisms, claims that for classical Athens (irrespective of what may be the case for other places and / or times) his own concentration on Athens' institutions is objectively right, because Athens was exceptionally institutionalised and his recognition of this does more justice to Athenian democracy than Ober's concentration on the *demos* and its ideology.

As a pluralist, I believe that questions of various kinds are worth asking; as a non-relativist, I believe that not all questions that may be asked are equally worth asking, but I am conscious that it is difficult to reach agreement as to which questions are most worth asking because our judgment may be affected both by our response to the subject which we are studying and by our response to ourselves and to the world in which we are living. In this particular case, I think that Hansen's questions about the machinery of the *polis* and Ober's questions about the ethos of the *polis* are both worth asking, that the questions which I asked about the Athenian *boule* and the questions which Connor wanted me to ask are both worth asking,[14] that interest in and knowledge of the answers to either one set of questions without interest in and knowledge of the other will impair our understanding of a complex phenomenon, that we are likely to misunderstand the phenomenon if we rely too much on one approach and use it to explain things which are better explained in other terms – 'better' not simply because another kind of explanation fits our own tastes or the concerns of our world better but because it does more justice to the phenomenon which we are trying to explain.

For any state, and not only for those at the most institution-alised end of the spectrum, finding out about the formal institutions and the rules governing their operation is an important part of finding out how the state worked, and I do not think that to believe that is merely to set up an 'ideological construct' for the study of history. But, of course, when we have found out that we have not found out the whole truth. Even for the formal institutions we need to know not only what the rules were but how the rules were used and abused in practice, and we need to discover as much as we can about the dynamics of political activity, both inside and outside the formal institutions, about the involvement and the non-involvement of individuals and of groups and classes of various kinds in public life. The questions which Hansen asks and those which Ober asks, my questions about the *boule* and those which Connor wanted to ask, are complementary.

Every approach has its dangers which its practitioners must guard against. Apart from legitimate 'intra-disciplinary de-bates over questions that are of primary significance within our paradigm', I have criticised Hansen for using the evidence in too mechanical a way to obtain right answers from it, and indeed for trying to make the Greek world appear tidier than it may in fact have been by assuming that there must be right answers to be found in some cases where I suspect that there may not.[15] One of the weaker chapters of Ober's *Athenian Revolution*, I believe, is the one in which he argues that what we call the reforms of Cleisthenes, in 508/7, resulted not so much from Cleisthenes' 'taking the people into his following'[16] as from a spontaneous popular uprising against Isagoras and the Spartan Cleomenes:[17] this fits Ober's view that the Athenian democracy was the achievement of an active *demos* which (to reverse Thucydides' comment on Pericles) was not led by the élite so much as led them,[18] but I think it builds far too much on Herodotus' innocent remarks that 'the *boule* resisted' Cleomenes and Isagoras and when they had occupied the Acropolis 'the rest of the Athenians came to an agreement [i.e. with the *boule*?] and proceeded to besiege them'.[19]

Drama as democratic performance

There has recently been a tendency, which I welcome, to view fifth-century Athenian drama not simply as 'literature' but as work performed at an Athenian festival – represented by many of the practitioners in this area as not so much a religious as a civic festival. (It is in fact an embarrassment to exponents of this kind of interpretation that the fullest ancient study of drama, Aristotle's *Poetics*, 'goes against the grain of all previous discussions of tragedy in virtually excising from the genre not only the Athenian democratic *polis*, but also the very abstract notion of a *polis*, and of the civic context, consciousness, and function of tragic drama'. E. Hall claims that 'in almost every text where tragedy is discussed or quoted in fifth-

and fourth-century Athens, including works by Aristotle other than the *Poetics*, such specificity [about the context to which tragedy belongs] is taken for granted'; and she argues that 'the *Poetics'* near-total displacement of the *polis* from tragedy seems to me to be an astonishingly original innovation, which adumbrates the incipient and future status of tragedy as an international art form. ... Tragedy was about to lodge a petition for divorce from the Athenian democratic *polis*.'[20] Her contrast is at any rate over-stated: there is a good deal of treatment of tragedy by Aristophanes, for instance, in the *Frogs* and elsewhere, which focuses on matters other than its civic context, and the view that the only legitimate way to study drama is to study it in its civic context is one for which it is hard to claim ancient support.) A great deal of work has been done in this area: I could not do justice to it here, and I think we need time for the dust to settle before we can satisfactorily combine what is valuable in these studies of drama produced by society to meet the needs of society with interpretations focusing in a more traditional way on playwrights and their audiences.[21]

However, I have been alarmed at the extent to which some scholars have tried to link the drama not merely with a *polis* which has the structures and institutions characteristic of a Greek *polis* but (as in my quotations from Hall, above) specifically with the democratic *polis*: it seems to me that the features of civic life and civic thought which underlie the performance of tragedy and comedy are features of *polis* life in general rather than of democracy in particular.[22] It is true that, even if the reforms of Ephialtes in 462/1 rather than those of Cleisthenes in 508/7 are best regarded as the defining stage in the creation of the Athenian democracy,[23] nearly all our surviving plays were written and performed in a democratic Athens. Democratic ideas can be found in Aeschylus' *Suppliants*, probably of 464/3;[24] his *Eumenides*, of 459/8, focused on the council of the Areopagus shortly after Ephialtes' removal of powers from that body; Athens under the rule of the legendary king Theseus is represented as democratic in Euripides' *Suppliants*, probably of the late 420s; and of course it is democratic Athens whose institutions and politics are among the subjects treated by Aristophanes and the other comedians.

But more than that is implied, for instance, by some contributors to a collection entitled *Nothing to Do with Dionysos?* and subtitled *Athenian Drama in its Social Context*. S. Goldhill in his contribution writes that the parade of the ephebes at the festival and what that signifies 'are all influenced by democratic *polis* ideology. ... The Great Dionysia ... is fundamentally and essentially a festival of the democratic *polis*.'[25] Elsewhere N.T. Croally writes not only that 'Greek tragedy is a discourse of the fifth-century Athenian *polis*' but that 'it must be viewed as reflecting the aims and methods of the democracy.'[26] H.P. Foley in a paper entitled 'Tragedy and Democratic Ideology' in fact alternates between the expressions 'democratic ideology' and '*polis* ideology'; but although she says, for instance, 'Obedience to the *polis* and its laws – just or unjust – was an important part of democratic ideology, even if it meant sacrificing family to city', that issue was not peculiar to the ideology of a *polis* which was democratic.[27] I think that more ought not to be implied: in so far as there is value in the study of drama as the product of the *polis* – and I think there is value in it, though not such overriding value as to invalidate other kinds of study – what matters is that it is the product of a Greek *polis*, with citizens and civic institutions, and it seems to me comparatively unimportant that the *polis* in question is democratic.

A recent book which continues this approach (but does not limit its attention to drama) is entitled *Performance Culture and Athenian Democracy*. The same excessive attention to the democratic constitution of classical Athens is betrayed, for instance, by a passage in Goldhill's introductory chapter: 'Thus, it can be instituted that the tribute of the allies should be paraded, ingot by ingot, in the theatre before the plays were performed at the Great Dionysia, a grand statement of the power and prestige of the polis, but, in turn, Isocrates ([VIII *On the Peace*], 82) can see this ritual as a way of the democratic state becoming more hated by its allies'[28] – but the reader who turns to the passage of Isocrates will find in it no reference to democracy. Again, T. Harrison in a book on Aeschylus' *Persians* has a chapter entitled 'Democracy and Tyranny', in which the contrast with which he is actually concerned is between *polis* institutions, not necessarily democratic, and despotism.[29]

So, as I thought Ober was indulging in wishful thinking when he invoked a popular uprising to explain Cleisthenes' reforms, I think Connor was indulging in wishful thinking when, in a paper entitled 'City Dionysia and Athenian Democracy', he not merely insisted that the conventional dating of Thespis' first performance and the institution of the Great Dionysia to the 530s is less than certain[30] but claimed that the institution of the festival would make better sense at the end of the sixth century, after the ending of the Pisistratid tyranny and the reforms of Cleisthenes, as a celebration of Athens' liberation and democracy.[31] I fear the influence of wishful thinking again when in a study of Athens' public buildings J.M. Hurwit claims that 'between 508 and 490, the democracy deliberately and thoroughly put its stamp upon the religious spaces of Athens'.[32]

The influence of democracy has been seen in other places where I suspect it ought not to be seen. The austerity of fifth-century Athenian casualty lists is sometimes thought to derive from the ethos of democratic Athens,[33] but P.A. Low has stressed that fifth-century casualty lists from oligarchic Boeotia are equally austere:[34] the ethos underlying these lists is that of the *polis*, but not specifically that of democratic Athens. H.S. Versnel has shown that Athenian religion is firmly anchored in the *polis*, but not specifically in the democracy.[35] Again, it has recently been claimed that fifth-century developments in Greek sculpture are to be attributed to democracy[36] – although those developments were not limited to democratic Athens and most of the sculptors were not Athenian citizens.

Grinding axes

If historians are too strongly conscious of the world for which they are writing, there is a danger that what they will give us will be 'an aberration or a mere product of the *Zeitgeist*'.[37] The journalist Stone wrote about the trial of Socrates in order 'to mitigate the city's crime and thereby remove some of the stigma the trial left on democracy and Athens'.[38] Roberts remarks that 'it would be gratifying to demonstrate decisively that journalists and moralists have experienced classical Athens very differently from professional historians. ... But no matter how much historians would like to delude themselves, these differences are frequently matters of degree rather than of kind.' She is arguing the relativist case, and her next sentence reads, 'Monarchists and republicans, slaveholders and abolitionists, feminists and traditionalists – we all have our axes to grind, though some of us grind them more gracefully than others'.[39] Now I have political views, as all people who think at all about the world they live in must have, but I am not conscious of having any axes to grind in my study of the ancient world,[40] and despite the claims of those who are ideologically committed and proud of it I believe that it is possible in principle to distinguish between scholarship that does have axes to grind in the modern world and scholarship that does not, though we are of course dealing with a spectrum, not with a clear-cut division into two categories.

Ober seems to me to go too far towards the axe-grinding end of the spectrum when he professes to 'make the Athenian democracy look both explicable in its own terms and an accessible tool for political analysis and action by those who are, or would be, citizens of democratic states'.[41] His opposition to Michels' 'iron law of oligarchy' is bound up both with a view that the present-day American democracy does exemplify that law but need not and should not, and with a view that Athenian democracy did not exemplify it and therefore provides a model for present-day America; and I have suggested that at any rate in his treatment of the reforms of Cleisthenes he has been led by this to a mistaken interpretation of what actually happened.[42] The present-day agenda is particularly evident in *Athenian Political Thought and the Reconstruction of American Democracy*, of which Ober was one of the editors. Several contributors are obsessed by the ways in which classical Athens failed to display qualities which we now value; Strauss emphasises for an America worried about continuing immigration that, if the democratic Athens of the late fifth and fourth centuries had a strongly exclusive view of its citizenship, earlier Athens was more willing to welcome immigrants as citizens, and through such devices as Cleisthenes' reorganisation of the citizen body found ways of integrating them as citizens;[43] Euben, another of the editors, both in this book and in the *Demokratia* edited by Ober and Hedrick tries to show that Plato was more of a democrat than he is usually taken to be – but is not likely to make many converts.[44]

Other scholars have drawn other lessons for today from their study of antiquity. P.A. Rahe in an avowedly unfashionable book, *Republics Ancient and Modern*, contrasts the Greek *poleis* with the beginnings and what he sees as the current predicament of the United States.[45] 'The *polis* ... was a moral community of men united as a people by a common way of life',[46] whose contribution to public life took precedence over freedom in their private life: its needs led to the discouraging of trade and private profit as causes of disunity. Sparta was most successful at that. 'Athens's Illiberal Democracy' was not what we should consider a democracy but merely enlarged the ruling class;[47] it left commerce largely to metics (free non-citizens), while the citizens concentrated on public concerns, warfare and honour just as elsewhere.[48] At the end of antiquity Christianity 'devalued the quest for office, for power and for glory, and it rendered citizenship and civic loyalty at best a secondary concern'.[49] Thinkers pointing the way to a secular view of humanity are traced from Machiavelli to Locke. One consequence of this secular view was a favourable attitude to science, material well-being and commerce: men like Paine and America's Founding Fathers were at first suspicious of commerce but came to accept it and to think that the ancients were excessively devoted to war and honour. Thus the American constitution was founded on the individualist aims of 'life, liberty and the pursuit of happiness'. It was shaped from the start by the need to accommodate southern states which retained slavery as well as northern states which were renouncing it, and Jefferson's presidency marked victory for supporters of states' rights against strong central government; 'as a commercial society founded on the marriage of trade and technology, the liberal republic tended to present itself as a congeries of special interests, not as a people united by a common cause'.[50] The result 'is and almost always has been a remarkably undemanding polity which provides little in the way of clear, direct moral guidance, and Americans have therefore been satisfied to live and let live and go their own way. ... It neither seeks to instill *homnoia* ['concord'] nor succeeds in doing so.'[51] Today the representative and accountable Congress abdicates its responsibility and leaves controversial decisions to the unrepresentative and unaccountable Supreme Court: Rahe wonders if the Americans will find when a crisis comes that they have enough in common to face it together.

I am not qualified to pronounce on Rahe's interpretation of the beginnings of the United States, or his diagnosis of today's ills. I am, however, worried by his use of ancient Greece. His emphasis on Sparta suits the lesson which he wishes to teach – within its restricted citizen body Sparta did indeed discourage commercial activity, concentrate on readiness for war and foster feelings of solidarity among the citizens – but Sparta in the classical period was self-consciously different from other states, and what he says of Greek *poleis* seems to me true but one-sided.

Another evaluation of democracy, ancient and modern, is to be found in a recent book by L.J. Samons, II, *Who Killed Socrates?*.[52] He complains that present-day Americans have made of democracy (and particularly of voting) an end, and indeed a religion, rather than a means to an end, and he suggests that the history of democratic Athens was often less than praiseworthy. Much of what we admire in Athenian culture, he believes, was the product of a *polis* but only incidentally of a democratic *polis*, and *eleutheria* ('freedom') and *isonomia* ('equality in law') were universal Greek ideals, not specifically Athenian or democratic ideals. The execution of Socrates was not a regrettable aberration but was all too typical of what democratic Athens was capable of; the democracy led to an excess of imperialism in the fifth century, and to reluctance to give up state pay and defend Athens against its enemies in the fourth;[53] but the evils of democracy were mitigated by other aspects of Athenian society, and Athenians asked what made Athens distinctive would lay much less stress on democracy than modern scholars tend to do. There are points in his argument with which I sympathise, for instance, his insistence that much which we associate with Athens because of our Athens-centred evidence is not specifically Athenian or democratic but is characteristic of the Greek states more generally;[54] but by the same token I think it may not be fair to blame the democracy for Athens' failure to pursue the policies which he regards as in its best interests.

Herodotus remarked that 'it is clear not just in one respect but generally that equality of speech (*isegorie*) is a worthwhile thing, since the Athenians under the tyranny were not superior in war to any of those living around them, but when freed from tyrants became by far the first' (V.78). V.D. Hanson in a book entitled *How the West Has Won* examines a series of battles from Salamis (where the Greeks defeated the invading Persians in 480), Gaugamela (Alexander the Great's last major victory over the Persians, in 331) and Cannae (the defeat by Carthage, in 216, from which the Roman citizens had the resilience to recover) to the Tet Offensive and the siege of Khesanh (in the United States' war in Vietnam, in 1968, where he thinks that the Americans on the spot were more successful than they were perceived as being, and that civic criticism led to more effective fighting in the remaining years of the war); and he takes up Herodotus' point, arguing that

> Western armies often fight with and for a sense of legal freedom. They are frequently products of civic militarism or constitutional governments and thus are overseen by those outside religion and the military itself. ... Western militaries put a high premium on individualism, and they are often subject to criticism and civilian complaint that may improve rather than erode their war-making ability. ... [In connection with the battle of Salamis] the moral drawn by Herodotus, for example, is unmistakable: free citizens are better warriors, since they fight for them-

selves, their families and property, not for kings, aristocrats or priests. They accept a greater degree of discipline than either coerced or hired soldiers.[55]

Freedom of expression may hamper military effectiveness in the short term, but (as even the Vietnam war demonstrates) it improves it in the long (esp. p. 438). Philip and Alexander of Macedon, of course, were not democrats, and Alexander's empire did not survive:

> Alexander the Great for a time created a deadly army by separating decisive battle from civic militarism; the Romans crafted an even deadlier military by returning the notion of shock battle to its original womb of constitutional government in ways far beyond even the Hellenic imagination. [p. 96]

Hanson thinks that because of the values it has cherished the West has become invincible, and the greatest threat to it would be not an attack from outside but a war within the Western camp;[56] and he concludes triumphantly:

> Western civilization has given mankind the only economic system that works, a rationalist tradition that allows us material and technological progress, the sole political structure that ensures the freedom of the individual, a system of ethics and religion that brings out the best in humankind – and the most lethal practice of arms conceivable. [p. 455]

The book has been written for a popular audience; and, at any rate on Salamis and Gaugamela, though Hanson is well read he inclines to naïve credulity on what the sources tell us. He also over-simplifies, I think, in the lessons which he draws from history. I am sure there is something in the claim that citizen soldiers, who can believe that a war is their war, fight with greater commitment and are more willing to suffer to attain an end which they approve of, and that military leaders who are subject to criticism may learn to avoid mistakes. But many other factors are relevant to success or failure, on particular occasions and in the long term, and I am not convinced that the glories of democracy provide the fundamental explanation of the course which the world's history has taken over the past 2,500 years.[57]

Direct use of history to teach moral and political lessons for our own time is not, I think, the way to go. It is important that, as far as we know, the ancient Greeks were the first people to have developed truly political institutions, through which *poleis* ('cities') became communities of *politai* ('citizens'), governed by their *politai*; and that first the Athenians and then some of the other Greeks decided that the best form of *politeia* ('city-governance') was a *demokratia*, in which political power was not monopolised by the well-born or the rich or the religious leaders but was shared among all the members of the *demos*.[58] It is enlightening, and stimulating of thought about our own world, to discover how the Athenians and the other Greeks formulated the principles of *polis*-governance and how they applied them in practice; and indeed to take note both of features which we from our standpoint may like, such as the direct involvement of the citizens in making decisions and in executing decisions, and of features which we may dislike, such as the exclusion from the citizen body of inhabitants other than free adult males of native descent. We can argue over the existence and the importance of features which particularly interest us: elaborate institutions and institutional rules, the dynamics of informal political activity; the extent to which democratic Athens tried to resist or succeeded in resisting the 'iron law of oligarchy'. In all of this, with Finley, 'we must acknowledge that other societies can act, and have acted, *in good faith* in moral terms other than ours, even abhorrent to us'[59] – and that in itself should be enlightening, and stimulating of thought about our own world.

But if we look too hard in ancient Greece for lessons for today's world we risk finding what we want to find rather than what was there. Without imagining that we can bring back to life in a post-modern age the corpse of a totally objective and dispassionate history, I still think that as historians we should try to place ourselves towards the objective and dispassionate end of the spectrum, because if we do that we are more likely to do better history, to do more justice to what we are studying:

> Ultimately, if political or moral aims become paramount in the writing of history, then scholarship suffers. Facts are mined to prove a case; evidence is twisted to suit a political purpose; inconvenient documents are ignored; sources deliberately misconstrued or misinterpreted.[60]

Indeed, if we make the effort to understand people different from ourselves on their terms, rather than force out of their context into ours features which happen to have a particular appeal for us, the effect of that kind of study of history on our ways of thinking about issues may also be more enlightening and for that reason more useful to us in our world. Paradoxically, I believe history is more useful when it does not try too self-consciously to be useful.

Notes

1. History

1. One writer among many who have stressed this is H.V. White: e.g. the essays collected in *The Content of the Form*, and cf. p. 14 with n. 93, below. For a recent study which 'trie[s] to steer a middle course between the extremes of postmodernist hyper-relativism on the one hand, and traditional historicist empiricism on the other', but with 'the weight of the argument ... directed against the post-modernists', see Evans, *In Defence of History*: quotation from Afterword in revised UK edition, 254-5.

2. Osborne, *Greece in the Making, 1200-479 BC.*

3. For a classic statement of the Logical Positivist position see Ayer, *Language, Truth and Logic.*

4. The old location: e.g. Travlos, *Pictorial Dictionary of Ancient Athens*, 72. The inscription and the new location: Dontas, *Hesperia* 52 (1983), 48-63.

5. For speculation on two alternative scenarios, if Artaxerxes III of Persia and Philip II of Macedon had not been killed in the first half of the 330s, or if history had taken its course then but Alexander the Great had not died in 323, see Toynbee, *Some Problems of Greek History*, 421-86.

6. 'Strenge Darstellung der Thatsache, wie bedingt und unschön sie auch sey, ist ohne Zweifel das oberste Gesetz'; 'wie es eigentlich gewesen': Ranke, *Geschichten der romanischen und germanischen Völker von 1494 bis 1535*, i, p. vi. Cf. 'wie sie gewesen' again, p. vii. The suggestion of Repgen, *Historisches Jahrbuch* 102 (1982), 439-49, that Ranke was translating Thuc. II.48.iii, 'I shall say what it [the plague at Athens] was like (ἐγὼ δὲ οἷόν τε ἐγίγνετο λέξω)' was refuted by Stroud, *Hermes* 115 (1987), 379-82. However, I owe to a hint from Dr J. Wisse a better precedent (but not necessarily one of which Ranke was conscious) in Lucian's *How to Write History* 39: 'The one duty of the historian is to say how it happened (τοῦ δὴ συγγραφέως ἔργον ἕν, ὡς ἐπράχθη εἰπεῖν)', which in its context is contrasted with displaying partiality.

7. Acton's letter of 12 March 1898 to contributors to the *Cambridge Modern History*, published in Acton, *Lectures on Modern History*, 315-18 app. i at 316. I have discussed the *Cambridge Histories* in a paper on the *Cambridge Ancient History* in *Histos* 3 (1999).

8. Cf. Evans, *In Defence of History* = *In Defense of History*, e.g. 114-15 = 98-9, 220-1 = 189-90, 231-2 = 198-9 (in the second passage quoting with approval Boghossian, *Times Literary Supplement* [13.xii.1996], 14-15 at 15). See for instance Ober's criticisms of Hansen (pp. 43-4, 74-5, below): he claims that Hansen's work appears to be objective, but it is in fact an ideological construct, which is to be rejected in favour of what we must presume to be Ober's own ideological construct.

9. I borrow the phrase 'artful reporter' from the title of a book by Hunter, *Thucydides, the Artful Reporter*. Notice what is said by Hornblower in the article on Thucydides in *OCD*[3], 1516-21 at 1520-1, to supplement the remarks of H.T. Wade-Gery repeated from the previous editions. For an extreme presentation of Thucydides as a writer with an axe to grind see Badian, in Allison (ed.), *Conflict, Antithesis and the Ancient Historian*, 46-91 with 165-81, revised in his *From Plataea to Potidaea*, 125-62 with 223-36; for an extreme presentation of Thucydides as a writer of literature rather than a searcher for truth see Woodman, *Rhetoric in Classical Historiography*, 1-69. For treatments which show how Thucydides' writing obeyed considerations of narrative appropriateness but which do not suppose that he was not interested in telling the truth see, e.g., Hornblower in Hornblower (ed.), *Greek Historiography*, 131-66 ch. v; Rood, *Thucydides: Narrative and Explanation*.

10. Armayor, *Harvard Studies in Classical Philology* 82 (1978), 45-62, 84 (1980), 51-74, *Herodotus' Autopsy of the Fayoum*;

Fehling, *Die Quellenangaben bei Herodot*, translated as *Herodotus and his 'Sources'*.

11. Ligota, *Journal of the Warburg and Courtauld Institute* 45 (1982), 1-13; quotations from pp. 3, 9-10.

12. See, for instance, the collection of essays edited by Cameron, *History as Text*.

13. See Moles, in Bakker et al. (edd.), *Brill's Companion to Herodotus*, 33-52 ch. ii: but the fact that we can detect resemblances between people and events which Herodotus mentions and people and events of the late fifth century is not, despite Moles' argument, sufficient to prove that he was writing with knowledge of those later people and events and with consciousness of the resemblances.

14. Ruskin, *Sesame and Lilies* (*Works*, ed. Cook & Wedderburn, xviii), 63 – and other remarks in the same vein.

15. For a modern formulation of it see Skinner, *History and Theory* 8 (1969), 3-53 at 48: 'The understanding of texts ... presupposes the grasp both of what they were intended to mean, and how this meaning was intended to be taken'. See also Hesk, *Deception and Democracy in Classical Athens*, 15-17, using the language but rejecting the conclusions of those who argue that it is impossible to penetrate behind The Text.

16. Cf. Rhodes, *Greece & Rome*[2] 41 (1994), 156-71.

17. *Metahistory* is the title of a book by H. V. White, on whom see p. 10 with 91 n. 1. He argues from a study of nineteenth-century historians that the writing of history is always preceded by the 'poetic' choice of a philosophy of history (pp. x-xi), that no one philosophy of history is demonstrably superior to the others, but 'the best grounds for choosing ... are ultimately aesthetic or moral rather than epistemological' (p. xii), and concludes (in opposition to what I have been arguing), 'The aged Kant was right, in short; we are free to conceive "history" as we please, just as we are free to make of it what we will' (p. 433).

18. See, for instance, Sullivan in *Arethusa* 8 (1975), 6 (in the Editorial of an issue devoted to Marxism and the Classics). On the different but related issue of history and theory see the recent book of Morley, *Writing Ancient History*, e.g. 23: 'There is no such thing

as a neutral, unproblematic definition of history; all definitions are working to someone's advantage at someone else's expense.'

19. For bibliography on these questions see Rhodes, *A Commentary on the Aristotelian Athenaion Politeia*, 251-3 with (1993) 773.

20. I cite not as remarkable but as typical a book which happens to be on my desk as I write this, Allen, *The World of Prometheus*, 37: 'My story about the ancient Athenian practices of punishing is intended to enhance our ability to think about punishing, politics, and freedom in the modern Anglo-American context.' Hall begins the Preface of *Inventing the Barbarian*, 'Every era finds in the study of the ancient world a context in which to express its own preoccupations' (p. ix).

21. See the article on slavery in *OCD*³, 1415-17: Greek by Cartledge, Roman by Bradley.

22. Interest in the concept of the Other is attributed by Cartledge, *The Greeks*, 2, particularly to E. Levinas.

For an especially striking instance of the focus on women, with reference to Athenian democracy, see Katz, in *Contextualizing Classics ... J.J. Peradotto*, 41-68, complaining (unjustifiably?) that 'the question of women's exclusion from political rights has been elided from the study of both women and democracy in ancient Athens'. Kurke, in Morris & Raaflaub (edd.), *Democracy 2500? Questions and Challenges*, 155-69 at 166 n. 2, has complained that 'Greek political history remains almost entirely the domain of male scholars', so that a study of Athenian democracy which concentrates on political matters and does not embrace, e.g., cultural history 'tends to exclude not only ancient women (as objects of study) but also modern women (as participants in the discussion)'. Ironically, she makes that complaint in a paper in which she argues, as I also do (cf. pp. 77-81, below) that it is a mistake to view Athenian tragedy as a specifically democratic phenomenon.

2. Democracy

1. Erythrae: Meiggs & Lewis 40 = *Inscriptiones Graecae* i³ 14, trans. Fornara 71; Miletus: Herrmann, *Klio* 52 (1970), 165-73 (editor's date adjusted in the light of Cavaignac, *Revue des Études Historiques* 90 [1924], 285-316 at 311-14).

2. [Xenophon], *Athenian Constitution*: the earliest use of the term 'Old Oligarch' I have found is Murray, *A History of Ancient Greek Literature*, 167-9.

3. Herodotus does not always use *demokratia* when writing of democracy: he uses it in cross references to the Persian debate and the Athens of Cleisthenes (VI.43.iii, 131.i) but not in his main treatment of either; when he uses it with reference to the Greek cities of Asia Minor at the beginning of the fifth century (IV.137.ii, VI.43.iii) he seems to mean constitutional government as opposed to tyranny.

4. Date: Bowra, *Pindar*, 410.

5. See, e.g., Ostwald, *Nomos and the Beginnings of Athenian Democracy*, esp. 96-136; Meier, *Die Entstehung des Politischen bei den Griechen*, 281-4 = *The Greek Discovery of Politics*, 161-2; Raaflaub in Kinzl (ed.), *Demokratia*, 1-54 at 46-51. In favour of the attribution of *demokratia* to Cleisthenes see, e.g., Fornara & Samons, *Athens from Cleisthenes to Pericles*, 40-50; Hansen, in *Ritual, Finance, Politics ... David Lewis*, 25-37.

6. This is the most natural interpretation of the Greek, but some scholars have felt unable to accept it. See Bruce, *An Historical Commentary on the Hellenica Oxyrhynchia*, 108 (following the original numbering in which this passage is 11.iv).

7. The abstract noun *probouleusis* is found only in a commentary, and not in a constitutional sense but with reference to Prometheus (schol. rec. on Pindar, *Olympians* vii.79-89 [III.i.263 Ábel]); but the verb *probouleuein* and the concrete noun *probouleuma* are used frequently in a constitutional sense.

8. Our sources do not give enough detail for certainty; I argued for this view of the intermediate régime in *Journal of Hellenic Studies* 92 (1972), 115-27.

9. Even in democratic states non-citizens were not allowed to own real property unless granted this right as a special privilege.

10. Cf. Rhodes with Lewis, *The Decrees of the Greek States*, 508-49 ch. v.

11. I say partly, because it is likely that the *Athenian Constitution*

was read and copied more than most of the other works in the collection, and so its chances of survival will have been better.

3. Democracy: Good or Bad?

1. In chs iii-v I have been greatly helped in the search for material by Roberts, *Athens on Trial: The Antidemocratic Tradition in Western Thought*. See also Ruschenbusch, in *Ritual, Finance, Politics ... D. Lewis*, 189-97.

2. E.g. his *Discourses*, I.2.xv-xvi (Lycurgus of Sparta produced a mixed constitution, which was durable; Solon of Athens produced a democracy, which was not); I.53 (the populace is easily misled by false hopes into seeking its own ruin).

3. Some of the local citizen assemblies called *Landsgemeinde* still exist: cf. p. 42, and see Hansen, *The Athenian Ecclesia*, 207-26; but Hansen in *Thinking Like a Lawyer ... J. Crook*, 138 n. 13, notes that three of the five which existed until recently have voted to abolish themselves.

4. Offler, in Bonjour et al., *A Short History of Switzerland*, 103-4.

5. See, e.g., the Petition of Right, 7.vi.1628 (Gardiner [ed.], *The Constitutional Documents of the Puritan Revolution, 1625-1660*, 66-70 no. 10); the Nineteen Propositions, 1.vi.1642 (249-54 no. 53); the Propositions of Newcastle, 13.vii.1646 (290-306 no. 66); the Heads of the Proposals, 1 viii.1647 (316-26 no. 71).

6. *Journals of the House of Commons*, vi.111 (4.i.1648/9: not in Gardiner).

7. Act abolishing King, 17.iii.1649 (Gardiner, 384-7 no. 88); Act abolishing House of Lords, 19.iii.1649 (387-8 no. 89); Act declaring England to be a Commonwealth, 19.v.1649 (388 no. 90).

8. See, for instance, *Areopagitica* (London, 1644: pp. 236-73 in the selection *John Milton*, edd. S. Orgel & J. Goldberg), which begins by quoting Euripides, *Suppliants* 438-41; *The Tenure of Kings and Magistrates* (London: M. Simmons, 1649; 2nd ed. 1650: pp. 273-307); *The Readie and Easie Way to Establish a Free Commonwealth* (London: L. Chapman, 1660; 2nd ed. 1660: pp. 330-53), which begins by quoting Juvenal i.15-16.

9. M. Reinhold, in Bolgar (ed.), *Classical Influences in Western*

Thought, AD *1650-1870*, 223-43 at 224-5 = his *Classica Americana*, 94-115 at 95.

10. E.g. A. Hamilton, in *The Federalist* (1787-8), ix (36-40 at 40 in the ed. of Beloff, on the Lycian federation); J. Madison, in xiv (61-6 at 62, on the contrast between the direct democracies of antiquity and a representative republic); Hamilton or Madison, in lxiii (321-8 at 323-5, insisting that there was a representative element even in ancient constitutions); J. Adams, *A Defence of the Constitutions of Government of the USA* (London: Dilly, 1787-8), reprinted in his *Works*, iv.472-92, 520-41 (considering Athens and Rome among 'Ancient Democratical Republics'), 542-9, 549-56 (considering Rome and Lacedaemon among 'Ancient Aristocratical Republics'), vi.100-8. A. Jackson, in 1828, was the first man to be elected President of the USA under the label Democratic.

11. L. de Jaucourt in Diderot & d'Alembert (edd.), *Encyclopédie, ou dictionnaire raisonné des sciences, des arts et des métiers*, iv.816-18 'démocratie'; quotation p. 816, 'Quoique je ne pense pas que la démocratie soit la plus commode et la plus stable forme du gouvernement'. i.817-18 'Athènes' is a very brief topographical account; xv.428-34 'Sparte ou Lacédémone' is a topographical account followed by an account of the 'Lycurgan' institutions.

12. Voltaire, *Dictionnaire philosophique / La Raison par alphabet*: not included in the earliest edd.; iii (= *Voltaire complet*, xl), 421-8 in the edition of 1821.

13. Pauw, *Recherches philosophiques sur les Grecs*, translated as *Philosophical Dissertations on the Greeks*; Barthélemy, *Voyage du jeune Anacharsis en Grèce*, translated as *Travels of Anacharsis the Younger in Greece*.

14. Cf. Vidal-Naquet, in Brisson, Vernant & Vidal-Naquet, *Démocratie, citoyenneté et héritage gréco-romain*, 40-1.

15. Mitford, *History of Greece*.

16. Turner, *The Greek Heritage in Victorian Britain*, 194. In 187-263 ch. v Turner surveys the treatment of Athenian democracy in Britain from Mitford to Zimmern and Grundy.

17. Paine, *The Rights of Man*, (London: Jordan, 1791-2), part II ch. iii; quotations pp. 229 and 233 in the World's Classics edition (1995).

18. Blackstone, *Commentaries on the Laws of England*, book I ch. ii (in vol. i). An early American instance A. Hamilton, letter to Gouverneur Morris, 19.v.1777, in his *Works*, vi.581-3 at 582.

19. De Tocqueville, *De la Démocratie en Amérique*, translated as *Democracy in America*: quotation from part II ch. i.15.

20. Winckelmann, *Gedanken über die Nachahmung der griechischen Werke in der Malerei und Bildhauerkunst*.

21. Macaulay, *Knight's Quarterly* 3 (August-November 1824), 117-28, 285-304 = *Complete Works*, xi.334-51, 365-93.

22. Grote, *Westminster Review* 5 (January-April 1826), 269-331: nominally a review of Clinton's *Fasti Hellenici*, but used 'to examine the merits and credibility of the most recent and celebrated book produced in this country on the subject, Mr. Mitford's history of Greece; a book to which Mr. Clinton continually refers with distinguished eulogy, and from which he appears to have borrowed all his views respecting Grecian society and institutions'); *History of Greece* (1st ed. 1846-56).

23. There are vigorous criticisms of Grote in the edition of Aristophanes' *Knights* by Rogers. Particularly relevant here is p. xviii n. 2: 'Grote was constitutionally incapable of holding an even balance between the demagogue [Cleon] and the more respectable and better educated Republicans. ... But much can be pardoned to Mr. Grote for his obvious sincerity, and for the extreme pain which it cost him to record anything to the discredit of a demagogue or a democracy.' The end of the Peloponnesian War and the oligarchy of the Thirty 'are somewhere wrapped up in a chapter entitled "From the battle of Arginusae to the restoration of Democracy in Athens after the expulsion of the Thirty", that is, from one democratic success to another democratic success.' P. xxvi: 'Grote's championship of Cleon against the unanimous verdict of the whole Greek world is rather the special pleading of a masterly advocate than the sober judgement of an impartial historian.'

24. Turner, *Greek Heritage*, 206-8.

4. Democracy: Fashions in Scholarship

1. Wallas, *Our Social Heritage*, 162.

2. For a short bibliographical survey with comments see Ehrenberg, *The Greek State*, 244-6, revised in 2nd ed., 256-9.

3. English translations of both of these were published: see Bibliography.

4. Lewis, *Acta of the Fifth International Congress of Greek and Latin Epigraphy*, 37 = his *Selected Papers in Greek and Near Eastern History*, 4.

5. 1st ed. 1871-88. This was written to replace, but marked a great advance on, the volume (ii) on the constitution in Becker's *Handbuch der römischen Alterthümer* (1843-67).

6. Busolt, *Griechische Staats-, Kriegs- und Privataltertümer* (1st ed. 1887); 3rd ed. entitled *Griechische Staatskunde* and partly ed. by Swoboda (1920/6).

7. Meyer, *Geschichte des Altertums*: on Grote, iii³, 228.

8. Wilamowitz, 'Von des Attischen Reiches Herrlichkeit', a *Festrede* for the 81st birthday of Kaiser Wilhelm I, in 1877, published in Kiessling & Wilamowitz (edd.), *Aus Kydathen*, 1-96 (cf. Lloyd-Jones, in the English translation of Wilamowitz's *History of Classical Scholarship*, p. xviii).

9. Roberts, *Athens on Trial*, 294-5 with 374-5 nn. 15-17.

10. Wade-Gery, *Journal of Hellenic Studies* 46 (1926), 293-7 at 294, reviewing the first of the books cited below.

11. See the preface of *Staatsgebiet und Staatsangehörige*, p. iii.

12. Kahrstedt, *Klio* 30 = ²12 (1937), 10-33; 31 = ²13 (1938), 1-32; 32 = ²14 (1939), 148-74; 33 = ²15 (1940), 1-12.

13. Ehrenberg, *Der griechische und der hellenistische Staat* (vol. iii.3 of Gercke & Norden's Einleitung in der Altertumswissenschaft, 1932, superseding Keil's *Griechische Staatsaltertümer* of 1912, ²1914); *Der Staat der Griechen* (1957/8; ²1965); translated as *The Greek State* (1960; ²1969).

14. Review of the English translation by Cartledge, *Classical Review²* 42 (1992), 99-101.

15. Review article by M.H. Hansen, *Classical Philology* 84 (1989), 137-48, beginning (perhaps unfairly to Kahrstedt), 'It may seem unbelievable, but this is in fact the first book in German on Athenian democracy since Wilamowitz's *Aristoteles und Athen* of

1893'; review by Rhodes, *Journal of Hellenic Studies* 107 (1987), 232.

16. Ehrenberg, *The Greek State*[2], 257 (modifying the wording but not the substance of the 1st ed.).

17. Slaves, women and the Delian League, *Les Démocraties antiques*, 133-6, 234-7; volatility of assembly, 183-7; bribery, 204-7.

18. Translated as *The Greek City and its Institutions* (cf. p. 39).

19. Lasserre, *La Science officielle: M. Alfred Croiset, historien de la démocratie athénienne* (a denunciation of Croiset's *Les Démocraties antiques*), with a preface by Maurras, pp. vii-xvi; preface reprinted with an introduction by the Marxist Hemmerdinger (referring to the book as 'un pamphlet que l'on peut détester, mais dont je crois avoir montre l'importance', 'a pamphlet which one can detest, but whose importance I believe I have shown') in *Quaderni di Storia* 2 / 4 (July-December 1976), 7-18: 'nos étrangers de l'interieur, juifs, meteques ou autres', pp. vii / 13; 'le gouvernement du nombre est d'essence pernicieuse', pp. xi / 15-16.

20. For recent French views of ancient democracy and what the modern world has made of it see the essays by Vidal-Naquet assembled in his *La Démocratie grecque vue d'ailleurs*, some of them translated as *Politics Ancient and Modern*; and, on the *Politiques de l'amitié* of Derrida (translated as *Politics of Friendship*) and on the roles of J.-P. Vernant, N. Loraux and J. Derrida in 'an explicit and ongoing dialogue between French hellenism and the politics of contemporary France', Leonard, *Proceedings of the Cambridge Philological Society*[2] 46 (2000), 45-78 (quotation p. 73).

21. M.-F. Stirbois, reported in *Journal Officiel de la République Française* (3.v.1990), 907-11, cited and discussed by Loraux, *Né de la terre*, 190-216 with 242-5, translated as *Born of the Earth*, 125-42 with 164-6 ch. xi.

22. Vidal-Naquet, in the Athenian section of Brisson, Vernant & Vidal-Naquet, *Démocratie, citoyenneté et héritage gréco-romain*, 7-41 at 37-41.

23. Greenidge, *A Handbook of Greek Constitutional History* and *Roman Public Life*.

24. Gilbert, *Handbuch der griechischen Staatsalterthümer*; vol. i^2 translated as *The Constitutional Antiquities of Sparta and Athens*.
25. Cf. pp. 37-8.
26. E.g. Pickard-Cambridge, *Demosthenes and the Last Days of Greek Freedom, 384-322 BC*, 75-6. (It is interesting to note that admiration for Thucydides has been so great that even scholars from whose own political stance we should not have expected it have tended to follow him in approving of Pericles and disapproving of Cleon.)
27. Grundy, *The Great Persian War and its Preliminaries*, 168-70; *Thucydides and the History of His Age*, <i>. 103-11 ('communistic' 106), cf. 169-211 ch. vii. Cf. the criticisms of Grote expressed about the same time by Rogers (p. 98 n. 23, above).
28. Cary, *History*^{2} 12 (1927/8), 206-14: quotations pp. 213, 214, 208.
29. Published in *History* 36 (1951), 12-28 = his posthumous *More Essays in Greek History and Literature*, 177-93.
30. Jones, *Athenian Democracy* (still in print).
31. Jones, *The Athens of Demosthenes* = *Athenian Democracy*, 23-38.
32. Brunt, *Dictionary of National Biography, 1961-1970*, 594-6 at 595.
33. Connor, *Classical Journal* 70 (1974/5), i. 32-40 at 32-3: the other works criticised are De Laix, *Probouleusis at Athens*; Geagan, *The Athenian Constitution after Sulla*. Connor's *Thucydides* begins with the impact on him and on his reading of Thucydides of the 1950s to 1980s, citing as crucial for him an article on Vietnam published in the *New Yorker* in 1968 (pp. 3-9), and ends with a comment on Thucydides from Brodie's *Strategy in the Missile Age* (p. 250), but still claims that his approach 'is not an aberration or a mere product of the *Zeitgeist* of the late twentieth century' (p. 243).
34. *The Decrees of the Greek States* was inspired by Swoboda, *Die griechischen Volksbeschlüsse* (Leipzig: Teubner, 1890); 'the failure of the *polis*' Browning, *Philologus* 120 (1976), 258-66 at 261, in a sympathetic review of the East German collection Welskopf (ed.), *Hellenische Poleis*; 'the destruction of Greek democracy' de Ste

Croix, *The Class Struggle in the Ancient Greek World*, chapter-heading p. 300 ch. v.3.

35. Rhodes, *Liverpool Classical Monthly* 3 (1978), 207-11; *Journal of Hellenic Studies* 106 (1986), 132-44; *Greece & Rome*² 43 (1996), 21-30. For the study of political activity as opposed to political institutions cf. pp. 44-6.

36. Osborne, *Demos: The Discovery of Classical Attica*; Whitehead, *The Demes of Attika*.

37. Osborne in Murray & Price (edd.), *The Greek City from Homer to Alexander*, 265-93 ch. xi. This theme has recently been taken further by N.F. Jones, *The Associations of Classical Athens*, on which see pp. 59-60.

38. Exploitation pp. 196-202, defence against critics (it did after all work) pp. 202-18. The book is reviewed by Hansen, *Classical Review*² 39 (1989), 69-76, who criticises it for playing down the difference between fifth-century and fourth-century institutions, and suggests that more attention should have been devoted to democratic ideology, which did not change as much as the institutions between the fifth century and the fourth.

39. Hansen, *Atimistraffen i Athen i Klassisk Tid*; revised version in English (published after two other works in English on judicial procedures), *Apagoge, Endeixis and Ephegesis against Kakourgoi, Atimoi and Pheugontes*.

40. E.g. *The Athenian Democracy*, 296-304.

41. The Copenhagen Polis Centre is producing two series of publications, edited by Hansen and others: Acts, published in the Royal Danish Academy's series Historisk-filosofiske Meddelelser Det Kongelige Danske Videnskabernes Selskab (beginning with 67 [1993]), and Papers, published as *Historia* Einzelschriften (beginning with 87 [1994]); a consolidatory book is to be published by OUP.

42. E.g. Hansen, *Was Athens a Democracy?*; *Polis and City-State*. In a recent paper, in *Thinking Like a Lawyer ... J. Crook*, 135-49, he examines schemes for taking advantage of technological possibilities to reintroduce a measure of direct democracy in the modern world, noting that they are based on five beliefs which underpinned the Athenian system, which he calls 'pillars of direct democracy'.

43. Ober, *Classical Philology* 84 (1989), 322-34; reprinted with

an introduction in his *The Athenian Revolution*, 107-22: quotations pp. 323-5 / 109-12; italicised words added *The Athenian Revolution*.

44. Hansen, *Classica et Mediaevalia* 40 (1989) [publ. 1993], 107-13.

45. Gelzer, *Die Nobilität der römischen Republik*; 'Die Nobilität der Kaiserzeit' (*Hermes* 50 [1915], 395-415); revised in his *Kleine Schriften*, i. 17-135 and 136-53; English translation of the two by Seager, *The Roman Nobility*, describing this as 'the most important book ever written' on Roman history (p. xii). Münzer, *Römische Adelsparteien und Adelsfamilien*, translated as *Roman Aristocratic Parties and Families*.

46. Michels, *Zur Soziologie des Parteiwesens in der modernen Demokratie*, translated as *Political Parties*: 'The Iron Law of Oligarchy' is a chapter heading in the English translation (part VI ch. ii, p. 393: 'Die Demokratie und das eherne Gesetz der Oligarchie', Teil VI Kap. ii, p. 351 in the 3rd German edition). Syme kept his citation of modern work to a minimum, and did not cite this book; I do not know whether he knew it.

47. Bowersock refers to the book as written under 'the ominous shadow of rising Fascism', but reports that the view of Augustus prompted by Syme's 'natural streak of rebellion' was present already in the unpublished draft, 'The Provincial at Rome', on which he worked in the late 1920s and early 1930s (*Proceedings of the British Academy* 84 ['1993 Lectures and Memoirs'], 539-63 at 547-9).

48. Several of the articles are republished in Sealey, *Essays in Greek Politics*.

49. A database for 360-322 had been attempted earlier by Sundwald, *Epigraphische Beiträge zur sozial-politischen Geschichte Athens*.

50. 'Pre-theoretical' p. vi.

51. Bentley cited p. x.

52. Bicknell, in various articles and *Studies in Athenian Politics and Genealogy*.

53. E.g. Rhodes, *Cambridge Ancient History*, v², 62-95 ch. iv.

54. Sealey, *Classical Philology* 59 (1964), 11-22 = his *Essays in Greek Politics*, 42-58; a later paper in *Classical Contributions ... M.F. McGregor*, 125-34. For a similar approach to developments in Athens see Davies, in Parker & Derow (edd.), *Herodotus and His World*, 319-35.

55. Ruschenbusch, *Historia* 15 (1966), 369-76; cf. his *Athenische Innenpolitik im 5. Jahrhundert v. Chr.*, arguing that constitutional changes to the end of the fifth century were normally made for reasons of foreign policy.

56. Sealey, *The Athenian Republic: Democracy or the Rule of Law?*. Another writer who believes that what the Athenians achieved in the fourth century was the rule of law is Ostwald, *From Popular Sovereignty to the Sovereignty of Law*.

57. For a response to that see, e.g., Rhodes, *Cambridge Ancient History*, v², 73-4; and notice such texts as Thucydides V.29.i, 31.vi (in 421 the Mantineans were glad to make an alliance with the Argives, *inter alia* because the Argives 'were democratically governed just like themselves', but the Boeotians and Megarians 'thought the Argives' democracy was less to their advantage, as they were oligarchically governed, than the Spartans' constitution').

58. Beginning with Denmark, which banned the slave trade in 1792 (to take effect in 1802).

59. Beginning with New Zealand, in 1893.

60. Self-government was granted to a single entity produced by the amalgamation of Upper Canada and Lower Canada in 1849; further provinces were added and the Dominion of Canada was created in 1867.

61. Dominion status was granted to India and Pakistan in 1947; India declared itself a republic in 1950, and Pakistan in 1956.

62. 'The slavery of legendary Greece ... not ... peculiarly harsh': Grote, *History of Greece*, ii.97-100 (12-vol. edition) = ii.37-9 (10-vol. edition); Sparta's helots 'no way inferior to any village population of Greece', but the elimination of a contingent of them (Thucydides IV.80.iii-iv) 'speaks volumes as to the inhuman character of the Lacedaemonian government': ii.373-80 = ii.291-7. One must take note of slaves (though ancient slavery was not as bad as modern) and women; because of that Athens cannot be called a democracy 'in the purest and most honourable sense of the term', though it can in a broader sense: Mill, *Edinburgh Review* 98 (July-

October 1853), 425-47 at 429-30, 439, reviewing vols ix-xi of Grote.

On these matters Mitford, far from being reactionary, had been ahead of his time: 'Among the many and great political evils incident to the allowance of slavery, two are eminent: First, a large, and generally the larger part of the population, is excluded from any interest in the country; and secondly, among the free people, between the rich and poor there can be little community', ch. iv §1; on helots and women in Sparta, ch. iv §3; on slaves in Athens, ch. v §4 (vol. i, pp. 182-3; 205-7, 213-15; 273-5 in 5-vol. ed. of 1808); and cf. de Tocqueville (p. 31 with 98 n. 19) on Athens as an 'aristocratic republic'. Cf. Turner, *Greek Heritage*, 196-7.

63. Cf. Winterer, *The Culture of Classicism*, 74-6.

64. Bradley in Abbott (ed.), *Hellenica*, 181-243 at 185-7 = [2]166-222 at 170-1; Grant, *Greece in the Age of Pericles*, who lamented that on account of the large number of slaves 'the democracies of the ancient world do not deserve the name according to our modern ideas', and 'in Greece the position of women was, according to our ideas, one of degrading subordination' (8-9).

65. *The Greek Commonwealth*, 180-97 ch. vii (quotation p. 191).

66. Gomme, *Classical Philology* 20 (1925), 1-25 = his *Essays in Greek History and Literature*, 89-115; followed by Kitto, *The Greeks*, 219-36.

67. See, e.g., de Ste Croix, *The Class Struggle in the Ancient Greek World*, 31-111 and *passim*.

68. Roberts, *Athens on Trial*, 259.

69. Roberts, *Athens on Trial*, 312.

70. Whittaker, *Proceedings of the British Academy* 94 ('1996 Lectures and Memoirs'), 459-72 at 464-5.

71. He insisted at the same time that 'we must acknowledge that other societies can act, and have acted, *in good faith* in moral terms other than ours, even abhorrent to us. Historical explanation is not identical with moral judgment': *Democracy, Ancient and Modern*, [1]57-8 = [2]95-6. Cf. 'Moral condemnation, no matter how well-founded, is no substitute for historical or social analysis': *Politics in the Ancient World*, 9.

72. *Historia* 8 (1959), 145-64 = his (ed.) *Slavery in Classical*

Antiquity, 53-72, and his *Economy and Society in Ancient Greece*, 97-115: quotation pp. 164 / 72 / 114-15.

73. In Garnsey & Whittaker (edd.), *Imperialism in the Ancient World*, 103-26 at 125-6.

74. Finley, *Democracy*, 23.

75. An influential book on the modern world is Schumpeter, *Capitalism, Socialism and Democracy*, which in 250-302 chs. xxi-xxiii replaces the 'classical theory of democracy' with a theory of competition for political leadership: the *demos* simply chooses between organised teams of candidates to govern, and there are massively effective barriers between the feckless decisions of individual citizens and the consequential choices of those whom they select to govern. This is cited in Finley, *Democracy*, 24 with 107 (175 in the 2nd ed.) nn. 25-6. A more recent book which has been influential for this approach to the study of politics is Parry, *Political Elites*.

76. Finley, *Politics*: quotation p. 9.

77. Padgug, *Arethusa* 8 (1975), 85-117.

78. Patterson, *Freedom*, i: Greece pp. 47-199 chs. iii-xi; quotation p. 91.

79. Stone, *The Trial of Socrates*: quotation p. xi.

80. Hanson, *How the West Has Won*, 50. On this book cf. pp. 86-8.

81. Forrest, *The Emergence of Greek Democracy*, 9-44 ch. i.

82. De Ste Croix, *The Class Struggle in the Ancient Greek World*, 278-326 ch. v. His view of the fifth-century empire was first expounded in *Historia* 3 (1954-5), 1-41, and follows a suggestion by Grote, *History of Greece*, vi. 9-10, 182-4 (12-vol. edition) = v. 149-51, 319-21 (10-vol. edition).

83. Stockton, *The Classical Athenian Democracy*: quotation 187 n. 19.

84. Osborne, *Dialogos* 1 (1994), 48-58.

85. Osborne, 'Changing Visions of Democracy'.

86. E.g. Cartledge, *History Today* 44. 4 (April 1994), 27-31; *Hermathena* 166 (Summer 1999), 5-29.

87. Beard, *Times Literary Supplement* (28.v.1999), 3-4, reviewing Millar, *The Crowd in the Late Roman Republic*.

5. Athenian Democracy and Us

1. Cf. Roberts, *Athens on Trial*, 176-9.

2. On the place of classics in American academic life from the late eighteenth century to the early twentieth see Winterer, *The Culture of Classicism*: on Everett and his contemporaries, 49-62.

3. See the obituary by Miller, *American Journal of Philology* 45 (1924), 97-100; and, on Gildersleeve and his contemporaries, Winterer, *The Culture of Classicism*, 110-17.

4. See Hedrick, forthcoming: I heard this paper at a colloquium in Cambridge in 1999, and thank Hedrick for letting me have a copy in advance of publication. The Athenian oath is preserved in a fourth-century inscription, Tod 204.5-20, trans. Harding 109; it is summarised by Lycurgus, *Against Leocrates* 76, of 330; and versions are given in the *Onomasticon* of Pollux (VIII. 105-6) and the *Florilegium* of Stobaeus (XLIII. 48).

5. E.g. Bloom, *The Closing of the American Mind*. Hanson & Heath, in *Who Killed Homer?*, and in an article with the same title in *Arion*[3] 5.2 (1997/8), 108-54, claim that some have tried to save classics, and their own jobs, by adopting either an egalitarian multi-culturalism or the view that the 'western tradition' and its Graeco-Roman origins are uniquely wicked, while those more traditionally minded have retreated into a dull pedantry.

6. This has been a particularly live issue in the United States, as in the late twentieth century people reacted against the courses in Western Civilisation introduced in many universities after the First World War. On post-modernism and multi-culturalism see Boghossian, *Times Literary Supplement* (13.xii.1996), 14-15 at 15. For some attacks on and defences of the canon of standard works in the western tradition see the issue devoted to this matter of *National Forum*, 69.3 (summer 1989). Fish, *There's No Such Thing as Free Speech, and It's a Good Thing Too*, castigates both extreme defenders of an unchanging canon and extreme relativists. Levine, *The Opening of the American Mind*, gives a sympathetic account of recent developments. Nussbaum in *Cultivating Humanity: A Classical Defense of Reform in Liberal Education* has written as a classicist in

favour of emphasising cultural diversity in higher education, whose purpose she sees as the production of good citizens.

7. Cf., among many publications which *Black Athena* provoked, in particular Lefkowitz & Rogers (edd.), *Black Athena Revisited*; Bernal, *Black Athena Writes Back*.

8. In what follows I am greatly indebted to discussion with Dr L. Rubinstein, though she is not to be blamed for the use which I have made of her ideas.

9. See for instance the bibliography of works in Danish and works in English (and some translations into other major languages) by M.H. Hansen in *Polis and Politics ... M.H. Hansen*, 617-30.

10. Ferguson, *The Treasurers of Athena*: quotation p. vii.

11. The reader will have noticed that that has been done in this book. This need has arisen partly because, as a result of changes in school and university syllabuses in the English-speaking world, it can no longer be assumed as it once could that those who study ancient history at a fairly advanced level will be able to read Greek and Latin and the principal modern European languages.

12. For the addition of contemporary concerns at beginning and end see, e.g., Walter, *An der Polis teilhaben*, and my review, *Gnomon* 69 (1997), 268-9; for an eye-catching title and an attempt by the publishers to suggest that a book is populist contrast, e.g., the dust jacket and the title with the actual book in the case of Hamilton, *Treasure Map*, and see my review, *Classical Review*² 52 (2002), 113-14.

13. 'For I am a Bear of Very Little Brain, and long words Bother me': Milne, *Winnie-the-Pooh*, p. 45 in the octavo edition.

14. Both expressions are, or at any rate were, sufficiently domesticated in English to be included in the edition which I possess of the *Concise Oxford Dictionary* (⁴1951).

15. I think of the book based on my own doctoral thesis, Rhodes, *The Athenian Boule*, which I should certainly be asked to recast in a more accessible form if I wanted to publish it now.

16. Cf. p. 49 with 105 n. 69.

17. McGregor, *The Athenians and their Empire*; Cargill, *The Second Athenian League: Empire or Free Alliance?*

18. *The Athenians and their Empire*, 166-77 ch. xvi.

19. Euben in a review article on Ober's *Political Dissent in Democratic Athens* remarks that he and Ober 'share the intellectual / political project of making Athenian political thought and democracy a presence in contemporary theoretical and political debates', and laments that 'the United States looks more like an ancient oligarchy than Athenian democracy' (*Polis* 17 [2000], 111-32 at 112).

20. Cf. pp. 43-4, 74-5. This quotation Ober, *Classical Philology* 84 (1989), 323 / *The Athenian Revolution*, 110 (where the first parenthesis is omitted).

21. The formulation of Raaflaub, *Political Theory* 11 (1983), 517-44 at 532.

22. Section heading, p. 332, using a term borrowed from A. Gramsci.

23. Cf. Roberts, *Athens on Trial*, 299. In connection with the first project see the exhibition catalogue Ober & Hedrick (edd.), *The Birth of Democracy*; Ober & Hedrick (edd.), *Demokratia: A Conversation on Democracies, Ancient and Modern*. The second project did not generate any publications.

I am not aware of any celebrations of the 2,500th anniversary of Solon's archonship in 1907/8. However, it is interesting to note that Cleisthenes' is not the only 2,500th anniversary which was celebrated in the late twentieth century: in 1971 the Shah of Iran celebrated what he called the 2,500th anniversary of the foundation of the Persian Empire, or, more precisely, of Cyrus II's proclamation in Babylon of freedom of worship and travel (in fact the year of the celebration was the 2,500th anniversary of the death of Cyrus), and the British Museum lent the Cyrus Cylinder to Iran for the celebrations. See *The Times* (8.x.1971), 8; (11.x), 6; (12.x), 8; (13.x), 6; (14.x), 8; (15.x), 1 (cont. p. 8) and 14 (Diary); (16.x), 5 and 13 (Letters); conference proceedings published in *Commémoration Cyrus ... 1971*; but against extravagant interpretations of the Cyrus Cylinder see A. Kuhrt, *Journal of the Study of the Old Testament* 25 (February 1983), 83-97. I am very grateful to Dr L.K. Allen for drawing my attention to this and showing me extracts from Iranian English-language newspapers.

24. Dunn (ed.), *Democracy: The Unfinished Journey, 508 BC to AD 1993*: his own chapter 239-66.

25. Among the many other publications generated by that anniversary, the following were written with enough of an eye on the present to deserve mention here: a series of articles by various authors in *History Today* 44 (1994; the issues for January-May, July, August); Morris & Raaflaub (edd.), *Democracy 2500? Questions and Challenges*, a book by classicists on classical subjects, but in which some of the contributors query the assumptions underlying that celebration; Smyth, Jones & Platt (edd.), *Bite the Ballot: 2,500 Years of Democracy* (the companion book to a Channel 4 television series), which is primarily concerned with the problems of democracy in the modern world, but at 19-21 reprints from *History Today* (above) an article by P. Cartledge on Athenian democracy, what has been made of it subsequently and what might and what should not be made of it, and at the bottom of the pages has time-lines running from *c.* 700 BC (the 'Lycurgan' reform in Sparta) to AD 1994 (multi-racial elections in South Africa, the electoral victory of the National Alliance in Italy).

26. The book is based on Protagoras, Thucydides and Democritus: on pp. 10-11 Farrar confronts the charge that what she presents is not 'a peculiarly democratic account' but 'a theory about the *polis* in general, or indeed about man in general, in the abstract'; but to my mind she succeeds in establishing the link with democracy only in the case of Protagoras.

27. Ober, *Échos du Monde Classique* 35 = ^{2}10 (1991), 81-96 = *The Athenian Revolution*, (123-)124-39 ch. ix: quotation p. 95 = 138 (last four words absent from *EMC*).

28. Euben, Wallach & Ober (edd.), *Athenian Political Thought and the Reconstruction of American Democracy*: reviewed by Rhodes, *Classical Review*^{2} 45 (1995), 317-18. Euben has written, *inter alia*, *Greek Tragedy and Political Theory*; *The Tragedy of Political Theory* (reviewed by Saunders, *Classical Review*^{2} 42 [1992], 67-9); *Corrupting Youth* (reviewed by Roberts, *American Journal of Philology* 120 [1999], 621-4).

29. Monoson has continued on this line in her *Plato's Democratic*

Entanglements (reviewed by Wallach, *Bryn Mawr Classical Review* 00-11-12, and by Goggans, *Polis* 18 [2001], 168-73).

30. Ober & Hedrick (edd.), *Demokratia*; quotation p. 3: reviewed by Rhodes, *Bryn Mawr Classical Review* 97-7-23 = 8 (1997), 664-7.

31. Cf. p. 43 with 102-3 n. 43.

32. Cf. above: a review article by Rhodes in *Polis* 15 (1998), 75-82.

33. See in particular Austin, *How to Do Things with Words*, 5. The formulation used in the English marriage ceremony is in fact 'I will', but Austin thought it was 'I do' (cf. 5 n. 2, by J.O. Urmson): his point is unaffected.

34. Ayer, *Language, Truth and Logic*[2], 102-20 ch. vi, cf. 33-45 ch. i and 5-16, 20-2: 'simply expressions of emotion' 102-3.

35. 'Enactment formula' is the terminology of Rhodes, *The Athenian Boule*, 64.

36. E.g. in Euben et al. (edd.), *Athenian Political Thought*, 149-71 at 160-1 = his *The Athenian Revolution*, (140-)142-60 at 151-2. In this instance it may be that when a majority had voted in favour the performative *edoxe*, 'It was resolved' (or perhaps the perfect *dedoktai*, 'It has been resolved', as in Aeschylus, *Suppliants* 601: see Rhodes, in Cairns & Knox (edd.), *Law, Rhetoric and Comedy in Classical Athens*, forthcoming) was used in the assembly, but the formula which we find in the prescripts of inscribed decrees is strictly the factual report that a performance of enactment has taken place.

37. In Hansen (ed.), *The Ancient Greek City-State*, 129-60 = his *The Athenian Revolution*, (161-)163-87 ch. xi.

38. Rawls, *A Theory of Justice*; cf. his *Political Liberalism*.

6. How to Study Athenian Democracy

1. Cf. Rhodes, *Durham University Journal*[2] 33 (1971/2), 148-9; *Polis* 15 (1998), 75-82; *Histos* 3 (1999).

2. Cf. pp. 59-60.

3. Ober, *The Athenian Revolution*, 6.

4. Cf. Samons, *Arion*[3] 5.3 (1997/8), 99-123 at 109; Wilson, *Classical Review*[2] 48 (1998), 374-6 at 376. *The Athenian Revolution*, 21-2 with 21 n. 4, 22 n. 6, cites Fornara & Samons, *From Cleisthenes*

to *Pericles*, as an example of 'historical scholarship that is thought and proclaimed by its authors to be staunchly "antitheoretical" ' (but which Ober claimes to be underpinned in fact by the 'iron law of oligarchy'); cf. 6-7 on 'naïve positivism'. Fornara & Samons are not naïve positivists; they insist that 'though it goes without saying that the ancient *testimonia* are the foundation of all modern reconstruction, ... it is nevertheless the case that they need constant reassessment, not only in the light of new knowledge, but because sometimes their amalgamation into ever more complex hypotheses, aiming at the categorical expansion of our knowledge, subtly or grossly distorts their ostensible meaning'; but they provocatively add, 'We largely ignore the work of those scholars whose interest in these underpinnings is secondary to their imposition on Athenian history of modern historical "models" inspired by the social sciences and strictly irrelevant to our own purpose of letting the sources speak for themselves' (p. xvii).

5. τῶν μελλόντων ποτὲ αὖθις κατὰ τὸ ἀνθρώπινον τοιούτων καὶ παραπλησίων ἔσεσθαι: Thucydides I.22.iv.

6. Ober, *Ancient History Bulletin* 3 (1989), 134-7 at 137 = *The Athenian Revolution*, 13-17 at 17.

7. Opp. citt.

8. Italicised words omitted *The Athenian Revolution*.

9. Cf. p. 65 with 110 n. 27.

10. *Classical Philology* 84 (1989), 322-34 = *The Athenian Revolution*, (107-)108-22.

11. 'an ideological' *Classical Philology*; 'a social' *The Athenian Revolution*.

12. Italicised passage omitted *The Athenian Revolution*.

13. Hansen, *Classica et Mediaevalia* 40 (1989) [publ. 1993], 107-13.

14. On Rhodes and Connor cf. p. 41.

15. Rhodes, e.g. *Journal of Hellenic Studies* 117 (1997), 236-8, reviewing two of the publications of the Copenhagen Polis Centre; *Eirene* 35 (1999), 33-40, on Hansen's treatment of one particular problem.

16. τὸν δῆμον προσεταιρίζεται: Herodotus V.66.ii.

17. Ober in Dougherty & Kurke (edd.), *Cultural Poetics in An-*

cient Greece, 215-32 = *The Athenian Revolution*, (32-)34-52 ch. iv. See Samons, *Arion*[3] 5.3 (1997/8), 99-123 at 110-15; Rhodes, *Polis* 15 (1998), 75-82 at 76; Wilson, *Classical Review*[2] 48 (1998), 374-6 at 375.

18. κατεῖχε τὸ πλῆθος ἐλευθέρως, καὶ οὐκ ἤγετο μᾶλλον ὑπ' αὐτοῦ ἢ αὐτὸς ἦγε ('he held the masses on a loose rein, and was not led by them so much as himself led them'): Thucydides II.65.viii.

19. ἀντισταθείσης δὲ τῆς βουλῆς ... Ἀθηναίων δὲ οἱ λοιποὶ τὰ αὐτὰ φρονήσαντες ἐπολιόρκεον αὐτούς: Herodotus V.72.ii.

20. Hall, in Silk (ed.), *Tragedy and the Tragic*, 295-309: quotations pp. 296, 297, 304-5.

21. For a general attack on the social interpretation of Athenian drama see Griffin, *Classical Quarterly*[2] 48 (1998), 39-61, of which pp. 47-50 are most relevant to my concern here; and in *Sophocles Revisited ... H. Lloyd-Jones*, 73-94 ch. v: for responses to the first see Seaford, *Classical Quarterly*[2] 50 (2000), 30-44; Goldhill, *Journal of Hellenic Studies* 120 (2000), 34-56 (insisting particularly strongly on democracy).

22. Cf. Kurke, in Morris & Raaflaub (edd.), *Democracy 2500?* 155-69 ch. viii; and, more generally on the confusion of the *polis* and the democratic *polis*, Eder, op. cit., 105-40 ch. vi, esp. 123-8; Boedeker & Raaflaub (edd.), *Democracy, Empire and the Arts in Fifth-Century Athens*; Samons, *Arion*[3] 8. 3 (2000/1), 128-57, esp. 138-40. I explore this theme at greater length in *Journal of Hellenic Studies* 123 (2003), forthcoming.

23. Cf., e.g., Rhodes, *Cambridge Ancient History*, v[2].87-92.

24. Cf. p. 19.

25. Goldhill in Winkler & Zeitlin (edd.), *Nothing to Do with Dionysos?*, 97-129 at 114; an earlier version *Journal of Hellenic Studies* 107 (1987), 58-76 at 68.

26. Croally, *Euripidean Polemic:* quotations pp. 1, 3.

27. Foley in Goff (ed.), *History, Tragedy, Theory*, 131-50; quotation p. 134 (expressing more pithily what is said by Sourvinou-Inwood, *Journal of Hellenic Studies* 109 [1989], 144).

28. Goldhill in Goldhill & Osborne (edd.), *Performance Culture and Athenian Democracy*, 1-29 ch. i at 8-9. In boring fact, the allies paid their tribute not in ingots but in coinage.

29. Harrison, *The Emptiness of Asia*, 76-91 ch. viii.

30. Thespis' first performance Olympiad lxi = 536-532, Suidas (θ 282) Θέσπις; apparently between 538 and 528, *Parian Marble* 239 A 43 (in Jacoby, *Die Fragmente der griechischen Historiker*); and other texts point to the time of Pisistratus: cf. West, *Classical Quarterly*[2] 39 (1989), 251-4. But 'in the city' is a less than certain phrase first introduced into the text of the *Parian Marble*. by A. Boeckh, and no text directly dates the establishment of the Great Dionysia: cf. Connor, cited in next note. Scullion, *Classical Quarterly*[2] 52 (2002), 81-101, expresses scepticism about all tragic dates earlier than 500.

31. Connor, *Classica et Mediaevalia* 40 (1989) [publ. 1993], 7-32; this and accompanying papers published also as a separate book, Connor et al., *Aspects of Athenian Democracy*, same pagination. Doubts about Connor's interpretation of the Dionysia are expressed by Raaflaub in *Polis and Politics ... M.H. Hansen*, 249-75 at 255-60; Burnett in *Gestures ... A.L. Boegehold*, forthcoming.

32. Hurwit, *The Acropolis*, 121-5 cf. 132: quotation p. 121. Contrast Whitley, *The Archaeology of Ancient Greece*, who, although he gives one of his chapters the title 'The Archaeology of Democracy: Classical Athens' (327-75 ch. xiii), and repeatedly mentions democracy in the section headings within that chapter, in his text is suitably cautious about connections between democracy and the buildings and objects found by archaeologists.

33. E.g. Meiggs & Lewis 33 = *Inscriptiones Graecae* i[3] 1147, beginning and end trans. Fornara 78: for association with democracy see for instance Loraux, *The Invention of Athens*, 15-76 ch. i ('The Funeral Oration in the Democratic City') at 22-3 ('The listing of the dead by *phylai* may not have been a specifically Athenian feature, but the democratic city was particularly careful to stress the closeness of the bond between the citizen and his tribe'); Goldhill, opp. citt. (p. 113 n. 25), 110-12 = 66-7 ('The values of democratic collectivity and the primacy of the city were stressed in a new form of memorial'); Osborne, *Past and Present* 155 (1997), 3-33 at 29 ('Democratic Athens took its opposition to claims based on lineage so far as to suppress patronymics on public monuments to the war dead').

34. *Inscriptiones Graecae* vii 585 (Tanagra), 1888 (Thespiae): Low, *World Archaeology* 35 (2003), forthcoming: paper read to

British Epigraphy Society, 11 November 2000. I am grateful to Dr Low for discussion and references.

35. Versnel, in Eder (ed.), *Die athenische Demokratie im 4. Jh. v. Chr.*, 367-87, with comments on Goldhill 375-7; cf. also Jameson, in Morris & Raaflaub (edd.), *Democracy 2500?* 171-95 ch. ix.

36. Cf. the exhibition catalogue, Buitron-Oliver (ed.), *The Greek Miracle: Classical Scuplture from the Dawn of Democracy* (e.g. the Introduction by Gage, 17-20); and the television series, *The Greeks: Crucible of Civilization* (see Bibliography). For a response see Hölscher, in Boedeker & Raaflaub (edd.), *Democracy, Empire and the Arts in Fifth-Century Athens*, 153-83 with 384-7 at 154-5; and cf. Whitley, cited p. 114 n. 32. For a flippant but not unfair reaction to the television series see Hoggart, *The Times* (15.i.2001), part ii p. 27; for a full critique of the series see Green, *Arion*[3] 8. 1 (2000/1), 159-73. Some of the more startling views expressed in the series may be found in print in Hanson, *How the West Has Won*, esp. 56-7 (on this book cf. pp. 86-8).

37. Connor, claiming not to have fallen into that trap: p. 101 n. 33, above.

38. Cf. p. 51.

39. Roberts, *Athens on Trial*, 308-9.

40. Cf. p. 71.

41. Cf. p. 60.

42. I must declare an interest: I have tried to cast doubt on the notion that Greek cities were to a serious extent 'acephalous' in *Historia* 44 (1995), 153-67, a paper formulated as a response not to Ober but to Pope, *Historia* 37 (1988), 276-96 at 277-82, 289-96.

43. Strauss in Euben et al. (edd.), *Athenian Political Thought*, 252-64.

44. Euben in Euben et al. (edd.), *Athenian Political Thought*, 198-226; in Ober & Hedrick (edd.), *Demokratia*, 327-59. A response to Euben by Barber in *Demokratia*, 361-75.

45. Rahe, *Republics Ancient and Modern* (I cite by the pagination of the original edition [1992]).

46. Op. cit., 30-1.

47. Cf. de Tocqueville, p. 31 with 98 n. 19.

48. Op. cit., 136-85 chs v-vi (Sparta); 186-218 ch. vii (Athens: quoting title of chapter).

49. Op. cit., 220.

50. Op. cit., 650.

51. Op. cit., 777.

52. Samons, *Who Killed Socrates?: Modern Lessons from Ancient Democracy*. Some of the themes of that book are foreshadowed in his article in *Arion* 8.3 (2000/1), 128-57.

53. Cf. the criticisms made of fifth-century Athens by Thucydides and of fourth-century Athens by Demosthenes.

54. Cf. pp. 77-81.

55. Hanson, *How the West Has Won* (cf. p. 51 with 106 n. 80): quotations pp. 21, 22, 47.

56. His book was written before the attacks on New York and Washington on 11 September 2001.

57. For a less ambitious, and more credible, attempt to derive lessons for today from the military history of the past see Strauss & Ober, *The Anatomy of Error: Ancient Military Disasters and Their Lessons for Modern Strategists*.

58. Cf. Finley, *Politics*, 51-3.

59. Cf. p. 105 n. 71.

60. Evans, *In Defence of History*, 219 = *In Defense of History*, 188.

Bibliography

Volumes of papers by various authors are listed under the editors / honorands when more than one paper is cited, under the particular author only when only one paper is cited. *Festschriften* are listed under the honorands, not the editors.

Acton, Lord, ed. Figgis, J.N. & Laurence, R.V. *Lectures on Modern History* (London: Macmillan, 1906).

Adams, J. *A Defence of the Constitutions of Government of the USA*, cited from his *Works* (Boston: Little, Brown, 1850-6).

Allen, D.S. *The World of Prometheus: The Politics of Punishing in Democratic Athens* (Princeton: Princeton UP, 2000).

Armayor, O.K. 'Did Herodotus Ever Go to the Black Sea?', *Harvard Studies in Classical Philology* 82 (1978), 45-62.

———— *Herodotus' Autopsy of the Fayoum* (Amsterdam: Gieben, 1985).

———— 'Sesostris and Herodotus' Autopsy of Thrace, Colchis, Inland Asia Minor and the Levant', *Harvard Studies in Classical Philology* 84 (1980), 51-74.

Austin, J.L. *How to Do Things with Words* (Oxford: OUP, 1962; [2]1975).

Ayer, A.J. *Language, Truth and Logic* (London: Gollancz, 1936; [2]1946).

Badian, E. *From Plataea to Potidaea* (Baltimore: Johns Hopkins UP, 1993).

———— 'Thucydides and the Outbreak of the Peloponnesian War: A Historian's Brief', in Allison, J.W. (ed.), *Conflict, Antithesis and the Ancient Historian* (Columbus: Ohio State UP, 1990), 46-91 with 165-81.

Barber, B.R. 'Misreading Democracy: Peter Euben and the *Gorgias*', in Ober & Hedrick (edd.), *Demokratia* (q.v.), 361-75.

Barthélemy, J.J. *Voyage du jeune Anacharsis en Grèce* (Paris: De Bure et al., 1788); translated by Beaumont, W., as *Travels of Anacharsis the Younger in Greece* (London: Robinson, 1791).

Beard, M. 'An Open Forum?', review of Millar, F. *The Crowd in the Late Roman Republic* (q.v.), *Times Literary Supplement* (28.v.1999), 3-4.

Becker, W.A. *Handbuch der römischen Alterthümer* (Leipzig: Weidmann, 1843-67).

Bentley, A.F. *The Process of Government* (Chicago: U of Chicago P, 1908; reissued Cambridge, Mass.: Harvard UP [Belknap Press], 1967).

Bernal, M. *Black Athena* (New Brunswick:Rutgers UP, 1987-91).

——— (ed. Moore, D.C.), *Black Athena Writes Back: Martin Bernal Responds to His Critics* (Durham, NC: Duke UP, 2001).

Bicknell, P.J. *Studies in Athenian Politics and Genealogy* (*Historia* Einzelschriften 19 [1972]).

Blackstone, W. *Commentaries on the Laws of England* (Oxford: Clarendon Press, 1765-9).

Bleicken, J. *Die athenische Demokratie* (Paderborn: Schöningh, 1985; [2]1994).

Bloom, A.D. *The Closing of the American Mind: How Higher Education has Failed Democracy and Impoverished the Souls of Today's Students* (New York: Simon & Schuster, 1987).

Boeckh, A. *Die Staatshaushaltung der Athener*, 2 vols (Berlin: Realschulbuchhandlung, 1817; [3]rev. Fränkel, M., Berlin: Reimer, 1886); translated by Lewis, G.C., as *The Public Economy of Athens* (London: Murray, 1828; [2]Parker, 1842).

Boedeker, D. & Raaflaub, K.A. (edd.), *Democracy, Empire and the Arts in Fifth-Century Athens* (Center for Hellenic Studies Colloquia 2. Cambridge, Mass.: Harvard UP, 1998).

Boghossian, P. 'What the Sokal Hoax Ought to Teach Us', *Times Literary Supplement* (13.xii.1996), 14-15.

Bibliography

Bolgar, R.R. (ed.), *Classical Influences in Western Thought,* AD *1650-1870* (Cambridge: CUP, 1979).

Bonjour, E., Offler, H.S. & Potter, G.R. *A Short History of Switzerland* (Oxford: OUP, 1952).

Bowersock, G.W., 'Ronald Syme, 1903-1989', *Proceedings of the British Academy* 84 ('1993 Lectures and Memoirs'), 539-63.

Bowra, C.M. *Pindar* (Oxford: OUP, 1964).

Bradley, A.C., 'Aristotle's Conception of the State', in Abbott, E. (ed.), *Hellenica* (London: Rivington, 1880), 181-243 = (London: ²Longman, 1898), 166-222.

Brisson, J.-P., Vernant, J.-P. & Vidal-Naquet, P. (responding to questions posed by Brisson, E.), *Démocratie, citoyenneté et héritage gréco-romain* (Paris: Liris, 2000).

Brodie, B. *Strategy in the Missile Age* (Princeton: Princeton UP, 1965).

Browning, R. 'The Crisis of the Greek City – A New Collective Study', review of Welskopf (ed.), *Hellenische Poleis* (q.v.), *Philologus* 120 (1976), 258-66.

Bruce, I.A.F. *An Historical Commentary on the Hellenica Oxyrhynchia* (Cambridge: CUP, 1967).

Buitron-Oliver, D. (ed.), *The Greek Miracle: Classical Sculpture from the Dawn of Democracy: The Fifth Century BC* (Washington, DC: National Gallery of Art, 1992).

Burnett, A.P. 'The First Tragic Contest: Revision Revised', in *Gestures: Essays in Ancient History, Literature and Philosophy in Honor of A.L. Boegehold* (Oxford: Oxbow, forthcoming).

Brunt, P.A. 'Jones, Arnold Hugh Martin (1904-1970)', *Dictionary of National Biography 1961-1970* (Oxford: OUP, 1981), 594-6.

Busolt, G. *Griechische Staats-, Kriegs- und Privataltertümer* (Handbuch der Altertumswissenschaft, IV.i.1. 1st ed. Nördlingen: Beck, 1887); 3rd ed. entitled *Griechische Staatskunde* and partly ed. by Swoboda, H. (Munich: Beck, 1920/6).

Cameron, A. (ed.), *History as Text* (London: Duckworth, 1989).

Cargill, J.L. *The Second Athenian League: Empire or Free Alliance?* (Berkeley & Los Angeles: U of California P, 1981).

Cartledge, P. 'Ancient Greeks and Modern Britons', *History Today*

44.4 (April 1994), 27-31; reprinted as 'Greek Lessons', in Smyth et al. (edd.), *Bite the Ballot* (q.v.), 19-21.

———— 'Democratic Politics Ancient and Modern: From Cleisthenes to Mary Robinson', *Hermathena* 166 (Summer 1999), 5-29.

———— Review of Meier, *The Greek Discovery of Politics* (q.v.), *Classical Review*² 42 (1992), 99-101.

———— *The Greeks* (Oxford: OUP, 1993; revised 1997; ²2002).

Cartledge, P. & Bradley, K.R., 'Slavery', *Oxford Classical Dictionary* (Oxford: OUP, ³1996), 1415-17.

Cary, M. 'Athenian Democracy', *History*² 12 (1927/8), 206-14.

Cavaignac, E. 'Les Dékarchies de Lysandre', *Revue des Études Historiques* 90 (1924), 285-316.

Clinton, H.F. *Fasti Hellenici*, vol. ii [first published] (Oxford: OUP, 1824).

Concise Oxford Dictionary (Oxford: OUP, ⁴1951).

Connor, W.R. 'City Dionysia and Athenian Democracy', *Classica et Mediaevalia* 40 (1989) [publ. 1993], 7-32.

———— 'The Athenian Council: Method and Focus in Some Recent Scholarship', review article on Rhodes, *The Athenian Boule*, De Laix, *Probouleusis at Athens* and Geagan, *The Athenian Constitution after Sulla* (qq.vv.), *Classical Journal* 70 (1974/5), i.32-40.

———— *The New Politicians of Fifth-Century Athens* (Princeton: Princeton UP, 1971).

———— *Thucydides* (Princeton: Princeton UP, 1984).

Connor, W.R. et al. *Aspects of Athenian Democracy* (*Classica et Mediaevalia* Dissertationes 11. Copenhagen: Museum Tusculanum P, 1990).

Croally, N.T. *Euripidean Polemic* (Cambridge: CUP, 1994).

Croiset, A. *Les Démocraties antiques* (Paris: Flammarion, 1909).

Commémoration Cyrus: Actes du congrès de Shiraz 1971 et autres études rédigées à l'occasion du 2500e anniversaire de la fondation de l'empire perse, 3 vols (Acta Iranica i.1-3. Leiden: Brill for Tehran: Bibliothèque Pahlavi, 1974).

Davies, J.K. *Athenian Propertied Families, 600-300 BC* (Oxford: OUP, 1971).

———— 'Democracy Without Theory' in Parker, R. & Derow, P. (edd.), *Herodotus and His World* (Oxford: OUP, 2003), 319-35.

Bibliography

——— *Wealth and the Power of Wealth in Classical Athens* (New York: Arno, 1981).

De Laix, R.A. *Probouleusis at Athens* (U. Calif. Pub. Hist. 83 [1973]).

Derrida, J. *Politiques de l'amitié* (Paris: Galilée, 1994); translated by Collins, G., as *Politics of Friendship* (London: Verso, 1997).

De Ste Croix, G.E.M. 'The Character of the Athenian Empire', *Historia* 3 (1954-5), 1-41.

——— *The Class Struggle in the Ancient Greek World* (London: Duckworth, 1981).

Diakov, V.N. & Kovalev, S.I. (edd.), *Histoire de l'antiquité* (Russian text Moscow: Gos. uchebno-pedagog, 1956; translated into French anonymously, Moscow: Éditions en Langues Étrangères, 1959).

Diderot, D. & d' Alembert, J.Le R. (edd.), *Encyclopédie, ou diction-naire raisonné des sciences, des arts et des métiers* (Paris: Briasson et al., 1751-72).

Dontas, G.S. 'The True Aglaurion', *Hesperia* 52 (1983), 48-63.

Dunn, J. 'Conclusion', in Dunn, J. (ed.), *Democracy: The Unfinished Journey, 508 BC to AD 1993* (Oxford: OUP, 1992), 239-66.

Eder. W. 'Aristocrats and the Coming of Athenian Democracy', in Morris & Raaflaub (edd.), *Democracy 2500?* (q.v.), 105-40 ch. vi.

Ehrenberg, V. *Der griechische und der hellenistische Staat* (vol. iii.3 of Gercke, A. & Norden, E. (edd.), Einleitung in die Altertums-wissenschaft: a third edition superseding Keil, *Griechische Staatsaltertümer*, q.v.); revised as *Der Staat der Griechen* (Leipzig: Teubner, 1957/8; ²Zurich: Artemis, 1965); translated as *The Greek State* (Oxford: Blackwell, 1960; ²London: Methuen, 1969).

Euben, J.P. *Corrupting Youth: Political Education, Democratic Culture and Political Theory* (Princeton: Princeton UP, 1997).

——— 'Democracy and Political Theory: A Reading of Plato's Gorgias', in Euben et al. (edd.), *Athenian Political Thought* (q.v.), 198-226.

——— 'Dissenting with Ober', review article on Ober, *Political Dissent* (q.v.), *Polis* 17 (2000), 111-32.

——— *Greek Tragedy and Political Theory* (Berkeley & Los Angeles: U of California P, 1986).

Bibliography

———— 'Reading Democracy: "Socratic" Dialogues and the Political Education of Democratic Citizens', in Ober & Hedrick (edd.), *Demokratia* (q.v.), 327-59.

———— *The Tragedy of Political Theory: The Road Not Taken* (Princeton: Princeton UP , 1990).

Euben, J.P., Wallach, J.R & Ober, J. (edd.), *Athenian Political Thought and the Reconstruction of American Democracy* (Ithaca: Cornell UP, 1994).

Evans, R.J. *In Defence of History* (London: Granta, 1997; revised ed., with Afterword responding to critics, n.d. [2001]) (a US edition, *In Defense of History* [New York: Norton, 1999], was revised from the 1st ed. and is differently paginated).

Farrar, C. *The Origins of Democratic Thinking: The Invention of Politics in Classical Athens* (Cambridge: CUP, 1988).

Federalist, The, ed. Beloff, M. (Oxford: Blackwell, 1948).

Ferguson, W.S. *The Treasurers of Athena* (Cambridge, Mass.: Harvard UP, 1932).

Fehling, D. *Die Quellenangaben bei Herodot* (Berlin: de Gruyter, 1971); translated by Howie, J.G., as *Herodotus and his 'Sources'* (Liverpool: Cairns, 1989).

Finley, M.I. *Democracy, Ancient and Modern* (London: Chatto & Windus, 1973; ²London: Hogarth / New Brunswick: Rutgers UP, 1985).

———— *Economy and Society in Ancient Greece* (London: Chatto & Windus, 1981).

———— *Politics in the Ancient World* (Cambridge: CUP, 1983).

———— (ed.) *Slavery in Classical Antiquity* (Cambridge: Heffer, 1960).

———— *The Ancestral Constitution* (Inaugural lecture, 4.v.1971. Cambridge: CUP, 1971).

———— 'The Fifth-Century Athenian Empire: A Balance Sheet', in Garnsey, P.D.A. & Whittaker, C.R. (edd.), *Imperialism in the Ancient World* (Cambridge: CUP, 1978), 103-26.

———— 'Was Greek Civilization Based on Slave Labour?', *Historia* 8 (1959), 145-64.

Fish, S. *There's No Such Thing as Free Speech, and It's a Good Thing Too* (New York: OUP, 1994).

Bibliography

Foley, H.P. 'Tragedy and Democratic Ideology: The Case of Sophocles' *Antigone*', in Goff, B. (ed.), *History, Tragedy, Theory: Dialogues on Athenian Drama* (Austin: U of Texas P, 1995), 131-50.

Fornara, C.W. & Samons, L.J., II, *Athens from Cleisthenes to Pericles* (Berkeley & Los Angeles: U of California P, 1991).

Forrest, W.G. *The Emergence of Greek Democracy* (London: Weidenfeld & Nicolson, 1966).

Francotte, H. *La Polis grecque* (Paderborn: Schöningh, 1907).

Gage, N. 'Introduction', in Buitron-Oliver (ed.), *The Greek Miracle* (q.v.), 17-20.

Gardiner, S.R. (ed.), *The Constitutional Documents of the Puritan Revolution, 1625-1660* (Oxford: OUP, ³1906).

Geagan, D.J. *The Athenian Constitution after Sulla* (*Hesperia* Supp. 12 [1967]).

Gelzer, M. 'Die Nobilität der Kaiserzeit', *Hermes* 50 (1915), 395-415.

———— *Die Nobilität der römischen Republik* (Leipzig: Teubner, 1912).

———— *Kleine Schriften* (Wiesbaden: Steiner, 1962-4).

———— the first two translated by Seager, R., as *The Roman Nobility* (Oxford: Blackwell, 1969).

Gilbert, G. *Handbuch der griechischen Staatsalterthümer* (Leipzig: Teubner, 1881-5; vol. i², 1893); vol. i² translated by Brooks, E.J. & Nicklin, T., as *The Constitutional Antiquities of Sparta and Athens* (London: Sonnenschein, 1895).

Glotz, G. *La Cité grecque et ses institutions* (Paris: La Renaissance du Livre, 1928); translated by Mallinson, N., as *The Greek City and its Institutions* (London: Kegan Paul, 1929).

———— *La Solidarité de la famille dans le droit criminel en Grèce* (Paris: Fontemoing, 1904).

Goggans, P. Review of Monoson, *Plato's Democratic Entanglements* (q.v.), *Polis* 18 (2001), 168-73.

Goldhill, S. 'Civic Ideology and the Problem of Difference: The Politics of Aeschylean Tragedy, Once Again', *Journal of Hellenic Studies* 120 (2000), 34-56.

———— 'Programme Notes', in Goldhill, S. & Osborne, R. (edd.),

Bibliography

Performance Culture and Athenian Democracy (Cambridge: CUP, 1999), 1-29 ch. i.

———— 'The Great Dionysia and Civic Ideology', *Journal of Hellenic Studies* 107 (1987), 58-76; revised in Winkler, J.J., & Zeitlin, F.I. (edd.), *Nothing to Do with Dionysos? Athenian Drama in Its Social Context* (Princeton: Princeton UP, 1990), 97-129 at 114.

Gomme, A.W. *Essays in Greek History and Literature* (Oxford: Blackwell, 1937).

———— *More Essays in Greek History and Literature* (Oxford: Blackwell, 1962).

———— 'The Position of Women in Athens in the Fifth and Fourth Centuries', *Classical Philology* 20 (1925), 1-25.

———— 'The Working of the Athenian Democracy', *History* 36 (1951), 12-28.

Grant, A.J. *Greece in the Age of Pericles* (London: Murray, 1893).

Green, P. 'Slag in the Crucible', *Arion*³ 8. 1 (2000/1), 159-73.

Greenidge, A.H.J. *A Handbook of Greek Constitutional History* (London: Macmillan, 1896).

———— *Roman Public Life* (London: Macmillan, 1901).

Griffin, J. 'Sophocles and the Democratic City' in *Sophocles Revisited: Essays Presented to Sir H. Lloyd-Jones* (Oxford: OUP, 1999), 73-94 ch. v.

———— 'The Social Function of Attic Tragedy', *Classical Quarterly*² 48 (1998), 39-61.

Grote, G. *History of Greece* (1st ed. London: Murray, 1846-56; 'new edition', in 12 vols, 1869/84, in 10 vols, 1888).

———— ('Institutions of Ancient Greece'), review of Clinton, *Fasti Hellenici*, ii (q.v.), *Westminster Review* 5 (January-April 1826), 269-331.

Grundy, G.B. *The Great Persian War and its Preliminaries* (London: Murray, 1901).

———— *Thucydides and the History of His Age* (London: Murray, 1911; reissued with the addition of a second volume Oxford: Blackwell, 1948).

Hall, E. *Inventing the Barbarian* (Oxford: OUP, 1989).

———— 'Is there a *Polis* in Aristotle's *Poetics*?' in Silk, M.S. (ed.), *Tragedy and the Tragic* (Oxford: OUP, 1996), 295-309.

Bibliography

Hamilton, A. *Works*, ed. Hamilton, J.C. (New York: Trow Francis, 1850-1).

Hamilton, R. *Treasure Map: A Guide to the Delian Inventories* (Ann Arbor: U of Michigan P, 2000).

Hansen, M.H. 'Athenian Democracy: Institutions and Ideology', review article on Bleicken, *Die athenische Demokratie, Classical Philology* 84 (1989), 137-48.

——— *Atimistraffen i Athen i Klassisk Tid* (Odense: Odense UP, 1973); revised version in English *Apagoge, Endeixis and Ephegesis against Kakourgoi, Atimoi and Pheugontes* (Odense: Odense UP, 1976).

——— 'Direct Democracy, Ancient and Modern', in *Thinking Like a Lawyer ... J. Crook* (*Mnemosyne* Supp. 231 [2002]), 135-49.

——— (ed.), *Introduction to an Inventory of Poleis* (Copenhagen: Acts of the Copenhagen Polis Centre 3 = Historisk-filosofiske Meddelelser Det Kongelige Danske Videnskabernes Selskab 74 [1996]).

——— 'On the Importance of Institutions in an Analysis of Athenian Democracy', *Classica et Mediaevalia* 40 (1989) [publ. 1993], 107-13.

——— *Polis and City-State: An Ancient Concept and its Modern Equivalent* (Copenhagen: Acts of the Copenhagen Polis Centre 5 = Hist. Fil. Medd. Dan. Vid. Selsk. 76 [1998]).

——— Review of Sinclair, *Democracy and Participation* (q.v.), *Classical Review*[2] 39 (1989), 69-76.

——— *The Athenian Assembly in the Age of Demosthenes* (Oxford: Blackwell, 1987, after earlier editions in Danish, 1977, and in German, 1984).

——— *The Athenian Democracy in the Age of Demosthenes* (Oxford: Blackwell, 1991, based on six more specialised fascicles in Danish, 1977-81; [2]London: Duckworth [Bristol Classical Paperbacks], 1999).

——— *The Athenian Ecclesia* (Opuscula Graecolatina 26. Copenhagen: Museum Tusculanum P, 1983).

——— 'The 2,500th Anniversary of Cleisthenes' Reforms and the Tradition of Athenian Democracy', in *Ritual, Finance, Politics ... D. Lewis* (q.v.), 25-37.

125

———— *Was Athens a Democracy?* (Copenhagen: Hist. Fil. Medd. Dan. Vid. Selsk. 59 [1989]).

———— *Polis and Politics: Studies in Ancient Greek History Presented to M.H. Hansen* (Copenhagen: Museum Tusculanum P, 2000).

Hansen, M.H. & Raaflaub, K.A. (edd.), *More Studies in the Ancient Greek Polis* (Papers of the Copenhagen Polis Centre 3 = *Historia* Einzelschriften 108 [1996]).

Hanson, V.D. *How the West Has Won: Carnage and Culture from Salamis to Vietnam* (New York: Doubleday, 2001).

———— *The Other Greeks* (New York: Free Press, 1985).

Hanson, V.D. & Heath, J. 'Who Killed Homer?', *Arion*³ 5.2 (1997/8), 108-54.

———— *Who Killed Homer?* (New York: Free Press, 1998).

Harrison, T. *The Emptiness of Asia* (London: Duckworth, 2000).

Hedrick, C.W. 'The Athenian Ephebe: Greek History and US Nationalism'; forthcoming.

Herrmann, P. 'Zu den Beziehungen zwischen Athen und Milet im 5. Jahrhundert', *Klio* 52 (1970), 165-73.

Hesk, J. *Deception and Democracy in Classical Athens* (Cambridge: CUP, 2000).

Hignett, C. *A History of the Athenian Constitution* (Oxford: OUP, 1952).

History Today 44 (1994).

Hölscher, T. 'Images and Political Identity: The Case of Athens', in Boedeker & Raaflaub (edd.), *Democracy, Empire and the Arts in Fifth-Century Athens* (q.v.), 153-83 with 384-7.

Hoggart, P. 'The Weekend's Viewing', *The Times* (15.i.2001), part ii p. 27.

Hopper, R.J. *The Basis of the Athenian Democracy* (Inaugural lecture, 30.i.1957. Sheffield: U of Sheffield, 1957).

Hornblower, S. 'Narratology and Narrative Techniques in Thucydides', in Hornblower (ed.), *Greek Historiography* (Oxford: OUP, 1994), 131-66 ch. v.

———— (part of article) 'Thucydides (2)', *Oxford Classical Dictionary* (Oxford: OUP, ³1996), 1516-21 at 1520-1.

Hunter, V.J. *Thucydides, the Artful Reporter* (Toronto: Hakkert, 1973).

Hurwit, J.M. *The Acropolis* (Cambridge: CUP, 1999).

Jameson, M.H. 'Religion in the Athenian Democracy', in Morris & Raaflaub (edd.), *Democracy 2500?* (q.v.), 171-95 ch. ix.

Jones, A.H.M. *Athenian Democracy* (Oxford Blackwell, 1957: still in print at Baltimore: Johns Hopkins UP).

———— *The Athens of Demosthenes* (Inaugural lecture, 23.i.1952. Cambridge: CUP, 1952).

Jones, N.F. *The Associations of Classical Athens: The Response to Democracy* (New York: OUP, 1999).

Kahrstedt, U. *Griechisches Staatsrecht*, i: *Sparta und seine Symmachie* (Göttingen: Vandenhoeck & Ruprecht, 1922).

———— *Staatsgebiet und Staatsangehörige in Athen* (Stuttgart & Berlin: Kohlhammer, 1934).

———— 'Untersuchungen zu athenischen Behörden':
    i. 'Areopag und Epheten', *Klio* 30 = [2]12 (1937), 10-33.
    ii. 'Die Nomotheten und die Legislative in Athen', *Klio* 31 = [2]13 (1938), 1-32.
    iii. 'Einige Instanzen aus der Rechtspflege', *Klio* 32 = [2]14 (1939), 148-74.
    iv. 'Bemerkungen zur Geschichte des Rats der Fünfhundert', *Klio* 33 = [2]15 (1940), 1-12.

———— *Untersuchungen zur Magistratur in Athen* (Stuttgart: Kohlhammer, 1936).

Katz, M. 'Women and Democracy in Ancient Greece', in *Contextualizing Classics: Ideology, Performance, Dialogue: Essays in Honor of J.J. Peradotto* (Lanham, Md.: Rowman & Littlefield, 1999), 41-68.

Keil, B. *Griechische Staatsaltertümer* (vol.iii.3 of Gercke, A. & Norden, E. (edd.), Einleitung in der Altertumswissenschaft. Leipzig: Teubner, 1912; [2]1914).

Kitto, H.D.F. *The Greeks* (Harmondsworth: Penguin, 1951).

Korovkin, F.P. *Ancient History: Textbook for the 5th Form* (Russian text, older editions *for the 5th & 6th forms*, more recent *for the 5th form*, Moscow: Prosveshcheniye, [4]1965; translated into English by Tabachnikova, O.G., Moscow: Prosveshcheniye, 1965).

Kuhrt, A. 'The Cyrus Cylinder and Achaemenid Imperial Policy', *Journal for the Study of the Old Testament* 25 (February 1983), 83-97.

Bibliography

Kurke, L., 'The Cultural Impact of (on) Democracy: Decentering Tragedy', in Morris & Raaflaub (edd.), *Democracy 2500?* (q.v.), 155-69 ch. viii.

Lasserre, P., with a preface by Maurras, C. *La Science officielle: M. Alfred Croiset, historien de la démocratie athénienne* (Paris: Nouvelle Librairie Nationale, n.d. [1909]).

Lefkowitz, M.R. & Rogers, G.M. (edd.), *Black Athena Revisited* (Chapel Hill: U of North Carolina P, 1996).

Leonard, M. 'The *Politiques de l'amitié*: Derrida's Greeks and a National Politics of Classical Scholarship', *Proceedings of the Cambridge Philological Society*[2] 46 (2000), 45-78.

Levine, L.W. *The Opening of the American Mind: Canons, Culture and History* (Boston: Beacon Press, 1996).

Lewis, D.M. 'Boeckh, *Staatshaushaltung der Athener*, 1817-1967', *Acta of the Fifth International Congress of Greek and Latin Epigraphy, Cambridge, 1967* (Oxford: Blackwell, 1971), 35-9.

——— *Selected Papers in Greek and Near Eastern History* (Cambridge: CUP, 1997).

——— *Ritual, Finance, Politics: Athenian Democratic Accounts Presented to David Lewis* (Oxford: OUP, 1994).

Ligota, C.R. ' "This Story is Not True": Fact and Fiction in Antiquity', *Journal of the Warburg and Courtauld Institute* 45 (1982), 1-13.

Loraux, N. *L'Invention d'Athènes: Histoire de l'oration funèbre dans la 'cité classique'* (Paris: Mouton for École des Hautes Études en Sciences Sociales, 1981); translated by Sheridan, A., as *The Invention of Athens: The Funeral Oration in the Classical City* (Cambridge, Mass.: Harvard UP, 1986).

——— *Né de la terre: Mythe et politique à Athènes* (Paris: Seuil, 1996); translated by Stewart, S., as *Born of the Earth: Myth and Politics in Athens* (Ithaca: Cornell UP, 2000).

Low, P.A. 'Remembering War in Fifth-Century Greece: Ideologies, Societies and Commemoration Beyond Democratic Athens', *World Archaeology* 35 (2003), forthcoming.

Macaulay, T.B. 'On Mitford's History of Greece' (q.v.), *Knight's Quarterly* 3 (August-November 1824), 285-304 = *Complete Works* (Albany Edition. London: Longman, 1898), xi.365-93.

——— 'On the Athenian Orators', *Knight's Quarterly* 3 (August-November 1824), 117-28 = *Complete Works* (Albany Edition. London: Longman, 1898), xi. 334-51.

McGregor, M.F. *The Athenians and their Empire* (Vancouver: U of British Columbia P, 1987).

Maurras, C. 'Préface' to Lasserre, *La Science officielle* (q.v.); reprinted with an introduction by Hemmerdinger, B., 'L'Action Française et la démocratie athénienne', *Quaderni di Storia* 2 / 4 (July-December 1976), 7-18.

Meier, C. *Die Entstehung des Politischen bei den Griechen* (Frankfurt a. M.: Suhrkamp, 1980); translated by McLintock, D., as *The Greek Discovery of Politics* (Cambridge, Mass: Harvard UP, 1990).

Meyer, E. *Geschichte des Altertums* (1st ed. Stuttgart: Cotta, 1884-1902); quotation from vol. iii^3 (Basel: Schwabe, 1954).

Michels, R. *Zur Soziologie des Parteiwesens in der modernen Demokratie* (Leipzig: Klinkhardt, 1911); ^{3}ed. Konze, W. (Stuttgart: Kröner, n.d. [1957]); translated by Paul, E. & C., as *Political Parties: A Sociological Study of the Oligarchical Tendencies of Modern Democracy* (London: Jarrold, 1915).

Mill, J.S. Review of Grote, *History of Greece*[1] (q.v.), vols ix-xi, *Edinburgh Review* 98 (July-October 1853), 425-47.

Millar, F. *The Crowd in the Late Roman Republic* (Jerome Lectures 22. Ann Arbor: U of Michigan P, 1998).

Miller, C.W.E. 'Basil Lanneau Gildersleeve, October 23, 1831 – January 9, 1924', *American Journal of Philology* 45 (1924), 97-100.

Milne, A.A. *Winnie-the-Pooh* (London: Methuen, 1926).

Milton, J. Cited from *John Milton*, edd. Orgel, S., & Goldberg, J. (The Oxford Authors. Oxford: OUP, 1990).

Mitford, W. *History of Greece* (London: Cadell & Davies, beginning 1784).

Moles, J. L. 'Herodotus and Athens' in Bakker, E.J. Jong, I.J.F. de & Wees, H. van (edd.), *Brill's Companion to Herodotus* (Leiden, Brill, 2002), 35-52 ch. ii.

Mommsen, T. *Römisches Staatsrecht* (1st ed. Leipzig: Hirzel, 1871-88).

Bibliography

Monoson, S.S. *Plato's Democratic Entanglements: Athenian Politics and the Practice of Philosophy* (Princeton: Princeton UP, 2000).

Morley, N. *Writing Ancient History* (London: Duckworth, 1999).

Morris, I. & Raaflaub, K.A. (edd.), *Democracy 2500? Questions and Challenges* (Dubuque, Iowa: Kendall-Hunt for Archaeological Institute of America, 1998).

Münzer, F. *Römische Adelsparteien und Adelsfamilien* (Stuttgart: Metzler, 1920); translated by Ridley, T., as *Roman Aristocratic Parties and Families* (Baltimore: Johns Hopkins UP, 1999).

Murray, G. *A History of Ancient Greek Literature* (London: Heinemann, 1897).

National Forum: The Phi Kappa Phi Journal (Baton Rouge: Louisiana State University), 69.3 (summer 1989).

Nussbaum, M.C. *Cultivating Humanity: A Classical Defense of Reform in Liberal Education* (Cambridge, Mass.: Harvard UP, 1997).

Ober, J. *Mass and Elite in Democratic Athens* (Princeton: Princeton UP, 1989).

———— 'Models and Paradigms in Ancient History', *Ancient History Bulletin* 3 (1989), 134-7.

———— *Political Dissent in Democratic Athens* (Princeton: Princeton UP, 1999).

———— *The Athenian Revolution* (Princeton: Princeton UP, 1996).

———— 'The Athenian Revolution of 508/7 BCE: Violence, Authority and the Origins of Democracy', in Dougherty, C. & Kurke, L. (edd.), *Cultural Poetics in Ancient Greece* (Cambridge: CUP, 1993), 215-32.

———— 'The Athenians and Their Democracy', review article on Farrar, *The Origins of Democratic Thinking*, Sinclair, *Democracy and Participation*, and Wood, *Peasant-Citizen and Slave* (qq.vv.), *Échos du Monde Classique* 35 = ^{2}10 (1991), 81-96.

———— 'The Nature of Athenian Democracy', review article on Hansen, *The Athenian Assembly* (q.v.), *Classical Philology* 84 (1989), 322-34.

———— 'The Polis as a Society: Aristotle, John Rawls and the Athenian Social Contract', in Hansen, M.H. (ed.), *The Ancient Greek*

City-State (Copenhagen: Acts of the Copenhagen Polis Centre, 1 = Hist. Fil. Medd. Dan. Vid. Selsk. 67 [1993]), 129-60.

Ober J., & Hedrick, C.W. (edd.), *Demokratia: A Conversation on Democracies, Ancient and Modern* (Princeton: Princeton UP, nominally 1996 but in fact 1997).

——— *The Birth of Democracy* (Athens: American School of Classical Studies at Athens, 1993).

Osborne, R. 'Athenian Democracy: Something to Celebrate?', *Dialogos* 1 (1994), 48-58.

——— 'Changing Visions of Democracy' (Inaugural lecture, Cambridge, 23.i.2002. To be included in a forthcoming volume).

——— *Demos: The Discovery of Classical Attica* (Cambridge: CUP, 1985).

——— *Greece in the Making, 1200-479 BC* (Routledge History of the Ancient World. London: Routledge, 1996).

——— 'Law, the Democratic Citizen and the Representation of Women in Classical Athens', *Past and Present* 155 (1997), 3-33.

——— 'The *Demos* and its Divisions in Classical Athens', in Murray, O. & Price, S. (edd.), *The Greek City from Homer to Alexander* (Oxford: OUP, 1990), 265-93 ch. xi.

Ostwald, M. *From Popular Sovereignty to the Sovereignty of Law* (Berkeley & Los Angeles: U of California P, 1986).

——— *Nomos and the Beginnings of Athenian Democracy* (Oxford: OUP, 1969).

Padgug, R.A. 'Classes and Society in Classical Greece', *Arethusa* 8 (1975), 85-117.

Paine, T. *The Rights of Man*, cited from the World's Classics edition (Oxford: OUP, 1995).

Parry, G. *Political Elites* (London: Allen & Unwin, 1969).

Patterson, O. *Freedom*, vol. i (all published. New York: Basic Books, 1991).

Pauw, C. de, *Recherches philosophiques sur les Grecs* (Berlin: Decker, 1787-8); translated by Thomson, J., as *Philosophical Dissertations on the Greeks* (London: Faulder, 1793).

Pickard-Cambridge, A.W. *Demosthenes and the Last Days of Greek Freedom, 384-322 BC* (New York: Putnam, 1914).

Pope, M. 'Thucydides and Democracy', *Historia* 37 (1988), 276-96.

Raaflaub, K.A. 'Democracy, Oligarchy and the Concept of the "Free Citizen" in Late Fifth-Century Athens', *Political Theory* 11 (1983), 517-44.

—— 'Einleitung und Bilanz: Kleisthenes, Ephialtes und die Begründung der Demokratie', in Kinzl, K.H. (ed.), *Demokratia* (Wege der Forschung, 657. Darmstadt: Wissenschaftliche Buchgesellschaft, 1995), 1-54.

—— 'Zeus Eleutherios, Dionysus the Liberator and the Athenian Tyrannicides: Anachronistic Uses of Fifth-Century Political Concepts', in *Polis and Politics ... M.H. Hansen* (q.v.), 249-75.

Rahe, P.A. *Republics Ancient and Modern* (Chapel Hill: U of North Carolina P, 1992; reissued in 3 paperback vols 1994; I cite by the pagination of the original edition).

Ranke, L. von, *Geschichten der romanischen und germanischen Völker von 1494 bis 1535*, i (Leipzig & Berlin: Reimer, 1824).

Rawls, J. *A Theory of Justice* (Cambridge, Mass.: Harvard UP, 1971).

—— *Political Liberalism* (New York: Columbia UP, 1993).

Reinhold, M., *Classica Americana: The Greek and Roman Heritage in the United States* (Detroit: Wayne State UP, 1984).

—— 'The Classics and Eighteenth-Century American Political Thought', in Bolgar, R.R. (ed.), *Classical Influences in Western Thought*, AD *1650-1870 ... iii. 1977* (Cambridge: CUP, 1979), 223-43.

Repgen, K. 'Über Rankes Diktum von 1824: Bloss sagen, wie es eignetlich gewesen', *Historisches Jahrbuch* 102 (1982), 439-49.

Rhodes, P.J. *A Commentary on the Aristotelian Athenaion Politeia* (Oxford: OUP, 1981, rev. 1993).

—— 'Aristophanes and the Athenian Assembly', Cairns, D.L. & Knox, R.A. (edd.), *Law, Rhetoric and Comedy in Classical Athens* (London: Duckworth with Classical Press of Wales, forthcoming).

—— 'How to Study Athenian Democracy', review article on Ober, *The Athenian Revolution* (q.v.), *Polis* 15 (1998), 75-82.

—— 'In Defence of the Greek Historians', *Greece & Rome*[2] 41 (1994), 156-71.

—— 'Nothing to Do with Democracy: Athenian Drama and the Polis', *Journal of Hellenic Studies* 123 (2003), forthcoming.

———— 'On Labelling Fourth-Century <Athenian> Politicians', *Liverpool Classical Monthly* 3 (1978), 207-11.

———— 'Personal Enmity and Political Opposition in Athens', *Greece & Rome*[2] 43 (1996), 21-30.

———— 'Political Activity in Classical Athens', *Journal of Hellenic Studies* 106 (1986), 132-44.

———— Review of Bleicken, *Die athenische Demokratie* (q.v.), *Journal of Hellenic Studies* 107 (1987), 232.

———— Review of Euben et al., *Athenian Political Thought* (q.v.), *Classical Review*[2] 45 (1995), 317-18.

———— Review of Finley, *The Ancestral Constitution* (q.v.), *Durham University Journal*[2] 33 (1971/2), 148-9.

———— Review of Hamilton, *Treasure Map* (q.v.), *Classical Review*[2] 52 (2002), 113-14.

———— Review of Hansen (ed.), *Introduction to an Inventory of Poleis*, and Hansen & Raaflaub (edd.), *More Studies in the Ancient Greek Polis* (qq.vv.), *Journal of Hellenic Studies* 117 (1997), 236-8.

———— Review of Ober & Hedrick (edd.), *Demokratia* (q.v.), *Bryn Mawr Classical Review* 97-7-23 = 8 (1997), 664-7.

———— Review of Walter, *An der Polis Teilhaben* (q.v.), *Gnomon* 69 (1997), 268-9.

———— 'Sparta, Thebes and *Autonomia*', *Eirene* 35 (1999), 33-40.

———— 'The "Acephalous" Polis?' *Historia* 44 (1995), 153-67.

———— *The Athenian Boule* (Oxford: OUP, 1972; rev. 1985).

———— 'The Athenian Revolution', *Cambridge Ancient History*, v[2] (Cambridge: CUP, 1992), 62-95 ch. iv.

———— 'The *Cambridge Ancient History*', *Histos* 3 (1999). (http://www.durham.ac.uk/Classics/histos/1999/rhodes/html)

———— 'The Five Thousand in the Athenian Revolutions of 411 BC', *Journal of Hellenic Studies* 92 (1972), 115-27.

Rhodes, P.J. with Lewis, D.M. *The Decrees of the Greek States* (Oxford: OUP, 1997).

Roberts, J.T. *Athens on Trial: The Antidemocratic Tradition in Western Thought* (Princeton: Princeton UP, 1994).

———— Review of Euben, *Corrupting Youth* (q.v.), *American Journal of Philology* 120 (1999), 621-4.

133

Bibliography

Rogers, B.B. *The Knights of Aristophanes* (London: Bell, 1910).

Rood, T. *Thucydides: Narrative and Explanation* (Oxford: OUP, 1998).

Ruschenbusch, E. *Athenische Innenpolitik im 5. Jahrhundert v. Chr.* (Bamberg: Aku, 1979).

———— 'Ephialtes', *Historia* 15 (1966), 369-76.

———— 'Europe and Democracy', in *Ritual, Finance, Politics ... D. Lewis* (q.v.), 189-97.

Ruskin, J. *Works*, ed. Cook, E.T., & Wedderburn, A., 39 vols (London: Allen, 1903-10).

Sagan, E. *The Honey and the Hemlock: Democracy and Paranoia in Ancient Athens and Modern America* (New York: Basic Books, 1991).

Samons, L.J., II, 'Democracy, Empire and the Search for the Athenian Character', review article on Boedeker & Raaflaub (edd.), *Democracy, Empire and the Arts in Fifth-Century Athens* (q.v.), *Arion*[3] 8.3 (2000/1), 128-57.

———— 'Mass, Elite and Hoplite-Farmer in Greek History', review article on Hanson, *The Other Greeks*, and Ober, *The Athenian Revolution* (qq.vv.), *Arion*[3] 5.3 (1997/8), 99-123.

———— *Who Killed Socrates?: Modern Lessons from Ancient Democracy* (Berkeley & Los Angeles: U of California P, forthcoming).

Saunders, T.J. Review of Euben, *The Tragedy of Political Theory* (q.v.), *Classical Review*[2] 42 (1992), 67-9.

Schoemann, G.F. *De Comitiis Atheniensium Libri Tres* (Greifswald: Mauritz, 1819); translated by Paley, F.A., as *A Dissertation on the Assemblies of the Athenians, in Three Books* (Cambridge: Grant, 1838: 'Advertisement' signed F.A.P.; for the identification of the translator see Stray, C.A. *Classics Transformed: Schools, Universities and Society in England, 1830-1960* [Oxford: OUP, 1998], 100 with n. 39).

Schumpeter, J.A. *Capitalism, Socialism and Democracy* (New York: Harper, 1942).

Scullion, S. 'Tragic Dates', *Classical Quarterly*[2] 52 (2002), 81-101.

Seaford, R. 'The Social Function of Attic Tragedy: A Response to Jasper Griffin', *Classical Quarterly*[2] 50 (2000), 30-44.

Sealey, R. 'Ephialtes', *Classical Philology* 59 (1964), 11-22.

Bibliography

————— 'Ephialtes, *Eisangelia* and the Council', *Classical Contributions: Studies in Honor of M.F. McGregor* (Locust Valley, NY: Augustin, 1981), 125-34.

————— *Essays in Greek Politics* (New York: Manyland, n.d. [1967]).

————— *The Athenian Republic: Democracy or the Rule of Law?* (University Park: Pennsylvania State UP, 1987).

Sinclair, R.K. *Democracy and Participation in Athens* (Cambridge: CUP, 1988).

Skinner, Q. 'Meaning and Understanding in the History of Ideas', *History and Theory* 8 (1969), 3-53.

Smyth, G., Jones, D., & Platt, S. (edd.), *Bite the Ballot: 2,500 Years of Democracy* (Supplement to *New Statesman and Society* 7 / 300 [29.v.1994]. London: Statesman and Nation, 1994).

Sourvinou-Inwood, C. 'Assumptions and the Creation of Meaning: Reading Sophocles' *Antigone*', *Journal of Hellenic Studies* 109 (1989), 134-48.

Stirbois, M.-F. Speech reported in *Journal Officiel de la République Française* (3.v.1990), 907-11.

Stobart, J.C. *The Glory that was Greece* (London: Sidgwick & Jackson, 1911; ⁴revised by Hopper, R.J., 1964).

Stockton, D. *The Classical Athenian Democracy* (Oxford: OUP, 1990).

Stone, I.F. *The Trial of Socrates* (Boston: Little, Brown, 1988).

Strauss, B.S. 'The Melting-Pot, the Mosaic and the Agora', in Euben et al. (edd.), *Athenian Political Thought* (q.v.), 252-64.

Strauss, B.S. & Ober, J. *The Anatomy of Error: Ancient Military Disasters and Their Lessons for Modern Strategists* (New York: St. Martin's P, 1992).

Stroud, R.S. ' "Wie es eigentlich gewesen" and Thucydides 2.48.3', *Hermes* 115 (1987), 379-82.

Sullivan, J.P. 'Editorial', *Arethusa* 8 (1975), 5-6.

Sundwald, J. *Epigraphische Beiträge zur sozial-politischen Geschichte Athens* (*Klio* Beiheft 4 [1906]).

Swoboda, H. *Die griechischen Volksbeschlüsse* (Leipzig: Teubner, 1890).

Syme, R. 'The Provincial at Rome', unpublished draft cited by Bowersock (q.v.).

Bibliography

———— *The Roman Revolution* (Oxford: OUP, 1939).

The Greeks: Crucible of Civilization (USA, An Empires™ Special: Atlantic Productions in Association with PBS and Devillier Donegan Enterprises [1999]; BBC 2 [January 2001]).

Tocqueville, A. de, *De la Démocratie en Amérique* (Paris: Gosselin, 1835-40); translated by Reeve, H., as *Democracy in America* (London: Saunders & Otley, 1835-40).

Toynbee, A.J. *Some Problems of Greek History* (Oxford: OUP, 1969).

Travlos, J. *Pictorial Dictionary of Ancient Athens* (London: Thames & Hudson for German Archaeological Institute, 1971).

Turner, F.M. *The Greek Heritage in Victorian Britain* (New Haven: Yale UP, 1981).

Versnel, H.S. in Eder, W. (ed.), *Die athenische Demokratie im 4. Jh. v. Chr.: Vollendung oder Verfall einer Verfassungsform? ... 3-7.viii.1992* (Stuttgart: Steiner, 1994), 367-87.

Vidal-Naquet, P. 'La Démocratie est née à Athènes', in Brisson, Vernant & Vidal-Naquet, *Démocratie, citoyenneté et héritage gréco-romain* (q.v.), 7-41.

———— *La Démocratie grecque vue d'ailleurs* (Paris: Flammarion, 1990); part translated by Lloyd, J., as *Politics Ancient and Modern* (Cambridge: Polity Press, 1995).

Voltaire, F.M.A. de, *Dictionnaire philosophique / La Raison par alphabet*: cited from *Voltaire complet* (Paris: Chez l'éditeur, 1821).

Wade-Gery, H.T. Review of Kahrstedt, *Griechisches Staatsrecht*, i (q.v.), *Journal of Hellenic Studies* 46 (1926), 293-7.

Wallach, J.R. Review of Monoson, *Plato's Democratic Entanglements* (q.v.), *Bryn Mawr Classical Review* 00-11-12.

Wallas, G. *Our Social Heritage* (London: Allen & Unwin, 1921).

Walter, U. *An der Polis teilhaben* (*Historia* Einzelschriften 82 [1993]).

Welskopf, E.C. (ed.), *Hellenische Poleis: Krise, Wandlung, Wirkung* (Berlin: Akademie-Verlag, 1974).

West, M.L. 'The Early Chronology of Attic Tragedy', *Classical Quarterly*[2] 39 (1989), 251-4.

White, H.V. *Metahistory* (Baltimore: Johns Hopkins UP, 1973).

———— *The Content of the Form: Narrative Discourse and Historical Representation* (Baltimore: Johns Hopkins UP, 1987).

Whitehead, D. *The Demes of Attika* (Princeton: Princeton UP, 1986).

Whitley, J. *The Archaeology of Ancient Greece* (Cambridge: CUP, 2001).

Whittaker, C.R. 'Moses Finley, 1912-1986', *Proceedings of the British Academy* 94 ('1996 Lectures and Memoirs'), 459-72.

Wilamowitz-Moellendorff, U. von, *Aristoteles und Athen* (Berlin: Weidmann, 1893).

———— translated by Harris, A., and edited by Lloyd-Jones, H. *History of Classical Scholarship* (London: Duckworth, 1982).

———— 'Von des Attischen Reiches Herrlichkeit', in Kiessling, A. & Wilamowitz-Moellendorff, U. von (edd.), *Aus Kydathen* (Philologische Untersuchungen, 1. Berlin: Weidmann, 1880), 1-96.

Wilson, P. Review of Ober, *The Athenian Revolution* (q.v.), *Classical Review*[2] 48 (1998), 374-6.

Winckelmann, J.J. *Gedanken über die Nachahmung der griechischen Werke in der Malerei und Bildhauerkunst* (Dresden & Leipzig: Walther, 1755).

Winterer, C. *The Culture of Classicism: Ancient Greece and Rome in American Intellectual Life, 1780-1910* (Baltimore: Johns Hopkins UP, 2002).

Wood, E.M. *Peasant-Citizen and Slave* (London: Verso, 1988).

Woodman, A.J. *Rhetoric in Classical Historiography* (London: Croom Helm, 1988).

Zimmern, A.E. *The Greek Commonwealth* (Oxford: OUP, 1911; [5]1931).

Index

When a word or name appears in parentheses, it will be found not in the text of the page cited but in a note to that page.

CPSIA information can be obtained
at www.ICGtesting.com
Printed in the USA
LVOW03s1651301117
558174LV00017B/287/P